DYNASTIES

Legendary Families of Stock Car Racing

DYNASTIES

Legendary Families of Stock Car Racing

Frank Moriarty

MetroBooks

MetroBooks

An Imprint of the Michael Friedman Publishing Group, Inc.

Moriarty Frank.
    Dynasties : legendary families of stock car racing / Frank Moriarty.
      p. cm.
    Includes index.
    ISBN 1-58663-180-2 (alk. paper)
1. Automobile racing drivers—United States—Family relationships. 2. Automobile
    racing drivers—United States—Biography. 3. Stock car racing—United States—History. I.
Title.

GV1032.A1 M66 2002
796.72'092'273—dc21
[B

                                    2001044934

Editors: Nathaniel Marunas and Rosy Ngo
Art Director: Kevin Ullrich
Photography Editor: Lori Epstein
Production Manager: Michael Vagnetti

Color separations by Radstock Repro
Printed in England by Butler & Tanner Ltd.

1 3 5 7 9 10 8 6 4 2

For bulk purchases and special sales, please contact:
Michael Friedman Publishing Group, Inc.
Attention: Sales Department
230 Fifth Avenue
New York, NY 10001
212/685-6610 FAX 212/685-3916

Visit our website:
www.metrobooks.com

Contents

INTRODUCTION

On February 18, 2001, the sport of stock car racing lost the man who was arguably it's greatest driver, Dale Earnhardt.

Earnhardt was charging hard in the Daytona 500, NASCAR's biggest and most prestigious race, which he himself had finally won for the first time—after a lifetime of trying—in 1998. On this day, though, it appeared victory was out of reach for him as he roared into the last turn at Daytona International Speedway. Instead, Michael Waltrip, driving for a race team owned by Earnhardt, was out front, thundering through the tri-oval toward the finish line with the checkered flag in sight and Earnhardt's son, Dale Earnhardt Jr., just behind him.

Tragically, Earnhardt would not be there to celebrate Waltrip's win in the Daytona 500. By now, everyone who follows stock car racing—and many who don't—are familiar with the sickening, slow-motion video replays of Dale's out-of-control Monte Carlo arcing across the speedway lanes as it followed a deadly trajectory toward the retaining wall.

Stock car racing was thrown into shock as the reality and enormity of the loss of Earnhardt began to sink in. The healing process was slow, and the wounds were continually reopened by the media's insatiable desire to find out what had gone wrong at Daytona. But healing began to take shape the week after Earnhardt's death.

Almost no one felt like racing on February 25 at North Carolina Speedway, but the old cliché "the show must go on" is law in the world of NASCAR. And when the show ended that day with the waving of the checkered flag, an amazing thing had happened—Steve Park, a young driver brought to the Winston Cup Series by Dale Earnhardt himself, had won the race in his yellow Dale Earnhardt Incorporated Chevrolet.

For the final time Dale Earnhardt acknowledges the cheers of thousands of fans. The green flag of his last race, the Daytona 500, was just minutes away.

On March 11, the Winston Cup Series returned to Atlanta Motor Speedway. In the same race a year earlier, Dale Earnhardt had won in a thrilling duel with Bobby Labonte, as his Richard Childress Racing Monte Carlo crossed the line mere inches ahead of Labonte's Pontiac. Faced with the daunting task of finding a replacement for Earnhardt as a driver in 2001, Childress turned to talented rookie Kevin Harvick to finish out the season in the car that had been driven by Dale.

As the laps in the Atlanta race wound down, spectators and millions of television viewers watched in amazement as Kevin Harvick held onto first place. Harvick was pressured by a rapidly closing Jeff Gordon, the former Winston Cup champion who had scored a win the week before. But when the flag waved, it was an exact repeat of the results from 2000—the Richard Childress Racing car, this time with Harvick at the wheel, holding off the competition by a foot.

The weeks went by, but a shadow loomed over the series as summer deepened, for on July 7 the stars of NASCAR would return to the track where Dale Earnhardt had been killed.

As teams arrived to prepare for Daytona's Pepsi 400, they faced incredible scrutiny from the media. "What was it like to be back at Daytona without Dale?" was the question that was asked over and over again.

Winless up to that point in 2001, Dale Earnhardt Jr. put out the word that he would not be available for interviews and would have no comment about returning to the track where his father had died. Instead, the driver everyone called "Junior" focused on preparing to race.

Junior, who had crossed the finish line just behind winner Michael Waltrip in the Daytona 500, was one of the fastest drivers in practice runs before the Pepsi 400. And when the green flag waved at Daytona as night fell, the careful preparation of Junior and his team began to show.

Either leading or running in the front pack all night, Junior was focused and determined. Even a late-race caution flag that sent everyone to the pits for service, resulting in Junior falling from first to sixth, didn't disrupt his concentration. When the green flag waved with just a handful of laps remaining, Junior simply charged back to the lead. It was the kind of performance that had made his father a NASCAR legend.

With Michael Waltrip almost glued to his rear bumper, with thousands of fans on their feet, with tears in the eyes of many who could barely believe what they were seeing, Dale Earnhardt's son won the first race at Daytona International Speedway since the tragedy in February. When he spoke after climbing from his Chevrolet, Junior's thoughts were of his father.

"He was with me tonight," Junior said. "I dedicate this win to him."

That simple statement, more than anything else, demonstrates the importance of family in NASCAR—from its earliest beginnings to the current day. Perhaps in no other sport is there such an ongoing legacy of talent being passed from generation to generation. On the pages that follow, the importance of strong family bonds to the sport will be in evidence over and over again in the remarkable stories of some of the most amazing drivers—whether brothers, sons, fathers, grandfathers, or even great grandfathers—ever to slip behind the wheel.

THE France *family*

In many ways, the National Association for Stock Car Auto Racing begins and ends with one family—the France family. Their story of the cultivation and amazing growth of the half-century-old motorsports sanctioning body is a tale of faith, control, determination, and, most of all, vision. That vision was doggedly pursued by the man who founded NASCAR, a man who became known as "Big Bill" France.

William Henry Getty France was born on September 26, 1909, in Washington, D.C. The son of a former farmer he displayed a keen

interest in automobiles—and their ability to go fast. He also grew interested in Anne Bledsoe a young nurse he met at a dance. In 1931, the couple were married.

Three years later, after the birth of a son also named William, the family moved south to Florida. Big Bill kept his hand in the automotive realm, opening an Amoco station in Daytona Beach. He also tried his hand at racing in local competitions, but he ventured into new territory when he promoted a race in 1938. The event, held on a course that ran partially on the beach and partially on a paved road, gave Bill France some very big ideas—ideas that would change the course of American racing.

France continued his promotional efforts for the next few years, but the eruption of World War II brought all recreational activities to a stop, and auto racing in Daytona Beach was no exception.

OPPOSITE PAGE: Bill and Anne France at an awards banquet, with sons Jim (front left) and Bill Jr. (far right). All four members of the family made immeasurable contributions to the world of motorsports.
THIS PAGE: Bill France knew what racers wanted—and appreciated their point of view—because he himself had racing in his blood. France is pictured here after winning a 1938 race that he had also promoted.

After the war, though, France analyzed the situation. The races on the beach and Highway A1A course were doing well again, but the American Automobile Association—which sanctioned races among special motorsports-only vehicles—had no interest in stock car racing. It was obvious to France that opportunity was knocking. He put out a call into the racing wilderness.

Racing really was a wilderness then—some promoters were honest, others were crooks, and competition rules varied wildly from location to location. France wanted to plant a seed that could grow into a national sanctioning body. Thirty-five men answered France's call, and assembled on December 14, 1947, at the Streamline Hotel in Daytona Beach.

Over the next three days a board of governors was assembled, with France serving as president. Car-builder Red Vogt came up with the name: NASCAR, National Association for Stock Car Auto Racing.

Two months later, the first NASCAR race was held, on February 15, 1948, at the Daytona beach and road course. Red Byron of Atlanta—one of the thirty-five men at the Streamline meetings—was

Big Bill and Bill Jr.—the father and son who guided NASCAR from its inception to heights unimaginable. It all began on the sands of Daytona Beach, where NASCAR is still head-quartered to this day.

the winner of the Winter 160. One week after Byron's win, NASCAR was incorporated.

The cars competing in the Winter 160 race had been governed under the rules for NASCAR's Modified division, which required full fenders and windshields on coupes, but allowed most anything else. On June 19, 1949, though, the roots of professional stock car racing took hold.

On that day, the first race of NASCAR's new Strictly Stock division was held. Strictly Stock cars were full-sized American-made passenger cars, with full bodies, and all parts required listing in the manufacturer's catalog for each model.

When the first race of the new division, held at North Carolina's Charlotte Speedway, was over, Jim Roper was declared winner after first-place finisher Glenn Dunnaway was disqualified for running on illegal springs. More importantly, though, NASCAR was on a path that would one day lead to the Winston Cup Series.

Not that the path was a smooth one. Bill France often had to control his sport with an iron fist, and he faced a multitude of challenges and problems. But France was confident that his vision was a sound one, and in the long run he was proven exactly right.

France was a brilliant promoter, and a master at recognizing opportunities. In 1951, Detroit's chamber of commerce was seeking a unique way to celebrate the city's 250th anniversary. France had the perfect idea—why not stage a 250-mile (402km) race, with one lap for each year of the city's history? The idea of an event based on the machinery that had made Detroit famous was irresistible, and the event was a tremendous success.

France had renamed his top series "Grand National" after the famed horse race, and with each passing year he took well-planned steps to elevate the sport of stock car racing to national popularity, moving it beyond its regional Southern roots.

Some people doubted France's wisdom, however, when he announced plans for a massive, two-and-a-half-mile (4km) superspeedway to be built in Daytona. But France brokered the complex deal and made another dream a reality. And when the first Daytona 500 was held on February 22, 1959, the last lap resulted in a publicity-generating photo finish. It was nearly three days after the race when France announced that Lee Petty had edged Johnny Beauchamp.

Other superspeedways were built, and France's march to sporting prominence gained momentum. Superstars emerged in his Grand National Series, men like Richard Petty, Ned Jarrett, Fireball Roberts, Junior Johnson, and Joe Weatherly. And with the competitors' prominence came television exposure.

To move the sport from beaches to superspeedways required construction of new racetracks, and the first and most important was South Carolina's Darlington Raceway. The man behind Darlington's birth, Harold Brasington (far left), looks on as Bill France makes a point.

Having telecast portions of NASCAR events since 1961, in 1970 ABC announced plans to broadcast nine races.

France's biggest deal, though, was yet to come. After he successfully negotiated with the tobacco giant, R.J. Reynolds came aboard as the sponsor of NASCAR's top division, and Grand National stock cars became Winston Cup cars.

With the financial backing of Winston, France had positioned his sanctioning body perfectly for a run at national prominence. After more than two decades of shepherding his vision, though, Bill France stepped aside from day-to-day control of NASCAR. The transition of power was seamless, however, because the head job was assumed by Big Bill's son, Bill France Jr.

The younger France had watched closely as Big Bill had dealt with triumphs and tragedies, and he wasted no time in building on the foundation crafted by his father.

A new wave of superstars began to emerge in the sport as the years passed. Names like Cale Yarborough, David Pearson, and Bobby Allison passed into the history book of NASCAR legends, while drivers like Bill Elliott, Darrell Waltrip, and Dale Earnhardt rose to the top of the Winston Cup Series.

Documenting the new wave of great NASCAR drivers—and further helping Bill France Jr. expose his sport to new audiences—was the ESPN cable television network. From its first race coverage on November 8, 1981, ESPN used innovative techniques for the next twenty years and helped make France's promotional duties easier. Joining ESPN in broadcasting NASCAR was CBS, a network which covered the Daytona 500 live, making NASCAR racing accessible to the millions without cable television hookups.

By 1995, three years after the death of his father, the younger France had cultivated Winston Cup attendance to attract six million fans at the series' thirty-one races.

At the turn of the millennium, though, France was diagnosed with cancer. Though he was forced for health reasons to step aside from NASCAR's offices while he recuperated, the culmination of his work and the work begun by his father fifty years before was manifested in a monumental new television deal. The multibillion-dollar agreement between NBC, Fox Television networks, and NASCAR was to begin in 2001, and would bring the sport to an even greater audience.

While Bill France Jr. battled cancer, his younger brother Jim—who had preferred to work behind the scenes as executive vice president and secretary of NASCAR, and president of International Speedway Corporation—was forced to step into the public eye. When Bill France Jr. resigned on November 28, 2000, Mike Helton, who had worked his way through the racing administration ranks leading to a stint as president of Talladega Superspeedway, was named president of NASCAR after several years serving first as vice president of competition and later as senior vice president and chief operating officer. Meanwhile, Brian France, the son of Bill Jr., was earnestly heading NASCAR's marketing department as executive vice president and generating tremendous new income. Brian's sister, Lesa France Kennedy, rose to executive vice president of International Speedway Corporation, overseeing the eleven racetracks controlled by the France's under the corporate spin-off from NASCAR.

After battling cancer, Bill France Jr. (right) returned to Daytona International Speedway in February 2000. Dale Earnhardt was delighted to see his old friend, and shared the joy of his win in the International Race of Champions event.

But the world had not seen the last of Bill France Jr. The first race of the new Fox television package ended in horrific tragedy when NASCAR's biggest star, Dale Earnhardt, was killed during the 2001 Daytona 500. The next day, at a national press conference, Bill France Jr. once again took charge of a crucial situation that threatened the sanctioning body his father founded.

Though the elevation of personnel like Mike Helton hints at a passing of the torch onto a new legacy, NASCAR and the world of stock car racing will forever be associated with one family, the France family.

THE Flock
Family

Many of NASCAR's legendary families have seen traditions carried on from father to son, but with the famed Flock family it was a single generation that made an unforgettable impact on the history of the sport. Brothers Bob, Fonty, and Tim all played crucial roles in the formative years of NASCAR and of professionally organized stock car racing as a whole.

Oldest brother Bob Flock, born April 16, 1918, was already well known in racing circles when Bill France took the first steps to form NASCAR. When France summoned the most important promoters, racers, and mechanics to join him at the Streamline Hotel in Daytona in December 1947, Bob Flock was among the now-legendary group invited.

Having played a key role in the formation of NASCAR, it's only fitting that Bob Flock should also be one of the organization's first victors. After competing in the first two NASCAR races ever held, Bob arrived at the third on August 7, 1949, in his Oldsmobile, determined to do more than finish far back in the pack. When the 200-mile (320km) event at Occoneechee Speedway, in Hillsboro, North Carolina, was complete, Flock had held off Gober Sosebee for the win.

Middle Flock brother Fonty, born March 21, 1921, almost beat his older brother to the family's first appearance in victory lane by nearly winning NASCAR's very first Strictly Stock race. Held on

OPPOSITE PAGE: Tim Flock cut a dashing figure in the early years of organized stock car racing, becoming one of the sport's first stars and helping to fill the grandstands with paying customers.
THIS PAGE: Bob Flock was an eyewitness to motorsports history off the track—and helped write some of that very same history through his exploits in competition. Bob was victorious in one of the very first NASCAR races.

June 19, 1949, at the Charlotte Speedway dirt track in North Carolina, the debut event of Bill France's stock car organization featured a field of thirty-three cars. Among them was Fonty Flock in a new Hudson. Flock gamely drove a good race, but didn't have quite enough to catch winner Glenn Dunnaway or runner-up Jim Roper. But Fonty's finishing position improved when Dunnaway's car was disqualified, moving the representative of the Flock family to second place in this legendary race.

Fonty was a perfect candidate for NASCAR competition, as he was an established Modified champion. He went on to score nineteen victories in 154 races over a nine-year NASCAR career.

Youngest Flock brother Tim, born May 11, 1924, who had run and placed fifth in the historic first NASCAR Strictly Stock race, nearly won the second. On July 10, 1949, in the first official NASCAR race held in Daytona Beach, Florida, Tim came within feet of winning on the treacherous beach and road course, finishing just behind a victorious Red Byron.

Tim Flock charges toward victory on April 2, 1950, in the tenth NASCAR Grand National race. His 1949 Lincoln held off the Oldsmobile of brother Bob at Charlotte Speedway in North Carolina, a three quarter-mile (1.2km) dirt track.

It was Tim who would go on to score the greatest triumphs for the Flock Family. He became the NASCAR Grand National champion twice, in 1952 and again in 1955. His winning ratio of 21 percent, achieved with thirty-nine race wins in 187 starts, is a record that still stands today.

The Flocks also brought something else to NASCAR: personality. A couple of snapshots: Fonty emerged from his car after winning the 1952 Southern 500 at Darlington Raceway clad in shorts and singing "Dixie." And Tim at one point took to racing with a rhesus monkey copilot he named Jocko Flocko. The man-primate arrangement ended when Jocko was struck by a small piece of debris during a race and went berserk, forcing Tim to make an unscheduled pit stop to remove Jocko from the cockpit.

Despite the high jinks, the Flocks' importance to the history of NASCAR is no joke. The three brothers combined to win sixty-three races, in the process elevating the family name to the pantheon of stock car racing.

What the well-dressed driver wears—Fonty Flock is a picture of sartorial splendor as he prepares to race on the old beach and road course in Daytona Beach, Florida.

THE
Baker
Family

While there is no disputing the impact of North Carolina's Baker family on the record books of stock car racing, there are some things that can't be reflected in a collection of statistics and records. One of those intangibles is toughness, a quality that father Buck Baker and son Buddy demonstrated time and again during their years of racing stock cars. And while many of the feats the Bakers accomplished on the track still top the assorted lists of records, when most race fans hear the name "Baker" they think of drivers who gave no quarter in their ferocious charges to the front of the pack.

Buck Baker is a member of the elite group of drivers who competed in the very first NASCAR Strictly Stock race in Charlotte, North Carolina, on June 19, 1949. Though Baker finished in eleventh place in that historic event, soon enough he would be the man in victory lane.

On April 12, 1952, Buck started the race at South Carolina's Columbia Speedway from the pole position. Two hundred laps later, Baker's Hudson Hornet was again at the front of the field, as the North Carolina driver held off Lee Petty to claim his first NASCAR Grand National victory.

Though the Columbia victory was Buck's only win in 1952, it was just the beginning of his illustrious racing career in stock car competition. In 1953 he crossed the finish line first in four races. One of those victories came at the prestigious Southern 500.

PREVIOUS PAGES: A jubilant Buddy Baker emerges from Ray Fox's Dodge after winning NASCAR's longest race, the 600-mile (965km) marathon at Charlotte Motor Speedway. Baker held off Donnie Allison to win the 1968 event.
THIS PAGE: Buck Baker in 1958, posing with his number 87 Chevrolet convertible. NASCAR's Convertible division was a four-year experiment, although top drivers like Baker, Joe Weatherly, and Lee Petty did try their hands at racing ragtops.
OPPOSITE PAGE: Father Buck Baker and son Buddy stroll side by side through the NASCAR garage area in 1967—a year when the series ran almost fifty races.

Peanut farmer Harold Brasington had visited Indianapolis Motor Speedway and decided he'd like to build his own speedway in Darlington, South Carolina. In 1950, the first Southern 500 was held on Brasington's new Darlington Raceway, after which the race began to gain the prestige that would make it an annual Labor Day tradition.

In the fourth running of the Southern 500, Buck Baker started seventh in his Olds 88 and was strong all day, leading more than 100 laps. But he had to battle hard against some of the greatest stars of early NASCAR competition, and Herb Thomas, Fonty Flock, and Fireball Roberts also took their turn at the front of the pack. But with just ten laps remaining in the dramatic event, Baker pushed his car past Thomas and clung to the lead to win the Southern 500.

In his great career, Baker would return to Darlington and triumph in the 1960 and 1964 Southern 500 races. He was a two-time NASCAR Grand National champion, winning the title consecutively in 1956 and 1957. In 636 starts in NASCAR's top division, Baker won forty-six times.

After retiring from competition, Baker eventually opened a highly regarded stock car racing school. Among the successful graduates of the school is modern superstar Jeff Gordon.

When Buck Baker retired from racing, the family name lived on in the racing exploits of his son, Buddy, who became known as one of the most aggressive NASCAR drivers ever to take the wheel.

It took Buddy Baker eight years of sporadic starts before he was able to make his way to victory lane. Finally, though, on October 15, 1967, it was Buddy Baker's day.

Driving a Dodge for well-known car owner Ray Fox, Baker had qualified in third for the running of the National 500 at North Carolina's Charlotte Motor Speedway. But the racing world was buzzing about the performance of Richard Petty, who had won ten straight races. Would his streak continue?

When the race got the green flag, Baker made his way to the lead on lap 114. The rest of the after-noon he battled for the top spot with such legendary drivers as Cale Yarborough, David Pearson, Bobby Isaac, and Dick Hutcherson. On lap 257, Baker pulled past Yarborough and assumed the lead for good. Petty's streak was over, and Baker's career was well underway.

Baker always seemed comfortable racing at Charlotte Motor Speedway, where he went on to win NASCAR's longest race—the Memorial Day weekend 600-mile (960km) event—three times.

Baker was also known for his fearless assaults on NASCAR's superspeedways: he won twice at Talladega, Alabama, and met success at NASCAR's other superspeedway in Daytona. In 1980, Buddy qualified on the pole for the Daytona 500 at a speed of just more than 194 miles per hour (310.4kph). Baker knew he had a car that could win NASCAR's biggest race, and when the event got underway Baker set course for the victory. He was pestered by 1979 Rookie of the Year Dale Earnhardt, but the young driver didn't have enough to run down the veteran Baker. When the checkered flag waved, Buddy Baker had won the Daytona 500 at a record pace of 177.602 miles per hour (284.2kph).

Buddy Baker set another significant record in March 1970 at Talladega Superspeedway. Driving a winged Dodge Charger Daytona prepared by Chrysler's Larry Rathgeb, Buddy Baker became the first stock car driver to turn a lap at more than 200 miles per hour (320kph).

After retiring from competition in 1994, Baker joined the staff of his father Buck's racing school and became a popular motorsports television commentator. Keeping his skills sharp, Baker still occasionally slips behind the wheel to test for Winston Cup teams.

OPPOSITE PAGE, TOP: At the superspeedway in Talladega, Alabama, Buddy Baker celebrates a new record. His blistering lap in Chrysler's new test car, the Dodge Charger Daytona, marked the first time a driver had broken the 200-mph (321.8kph) barrier during an officially timed lap.

OPPOSITE PAGE, BOTTOM: Buddy Baker's crew changes tires on his Oldsmobile in the midst of racing action at Dover, Delaware. Pit stops that seemed swift during the 1980s would be judged disastrously slow by today's standards. THIS PAGE: Buddy Baker's association with the legendary Wood Brothers team paid off on July 4, 1983, a day when the number 21 car was unstoppable. Here, Baker leads Bobby Allison's 22 car and Terry Labonte's 44 early in the event.

THE Petty Family

THIS PAGE: Lee Petty was the patriarch of the Petty dynasty. Seen here in 1956, he proudly stands beside his car.
OPPOSITE PAGE: Adam Petty was in position to become the next Petty family member to make his mark in the record books of NASCAR. Pictured here at Nashville Speedway on April 8, 2000, Adam ranked as the third fastest during the first practice run for the eighth race of the Busch Series season.

If you want to sum up the sport of stock car racing in a single word, that word would be "Petty." Of all the famous names and colorful legends that make up the history of NASCAR, there is none that carries more weight or has had a greater historical impact than North Carolina's racing Pettys. Included in the saga of the Pettys' NASCAR association, which continues after more than five decades, are triumph, determination, tragedy, anger, humor, and many, many hard-fought individual victories and series championships. It's safe to say there will never be another family in racing like this incredible clan, which helped found the sport, nurture it through its adolescence, and rose with it to the greatest levels of achievement and popularity.

The Petty stock car racing dynasty has roots that stretch way back, deep into stock car racing history. In fact, you can't go back much further than the first NASCAR Strictly Stock race, held on June 19, 1949, at Charlotte Speedway in North Carolina.

To make the newly formed NASCAR a success, Big Bill France knew he had to field cars that the fans in the stands could easily identify with. No one could have imagined that this Strictly Stock race would leave in its wake a chain of events leading directly to today's Winston Cup Series. Of course, they could easily imagine that pocketing the winner's purse of $2,000 would be nice—not to mention owning the bragging rights that would come along with victory in the race.

OPPOSITE PAGE, TOP: One of the great moments in NASCAR racing, and one Daytona 500 in which The King did not emerge victorious. Gunning for the victory in 1976, Richard Petty and arch-rival David Pearson spun out in sight of the checkered flag. Pearson recovered just in time to win.

OPPOSITE PAGE, BOTTOM LEFT: Richard Petty at Daytona in 1989 sits on a throne suitable for NASCAR's King, comfortably ensconced amidst a stack of Goodyear tires and other tools of his trade.

OPPOSITE PAGE, BOTTOM RIGHT: For decades of NASCAR history, Richard Petty was symbolic of his sport. So familiar was Richard's presence that the shade of blue that his cars bore became known as "Petty blue."

Among the competitors in the 200-lap event was a young man who had prepped his Buick Roadmaster in a barn on his farm in Randleman, North Carolina. Lee Petty started the race in ninth place, but on lap 107 he learned a hard lesson about stock car racing when he rolled the vehicle, crashing out of the event. Petty's accident was the only crash in the historic race. Fortunately, Lee Petty would soon find far better fortune on the racetrack.

In just the seventh Strictly Stock race, at Pennsylvania's Heidelberg Speedway, near Pittsburgh, on October 2, 1949, Lee saw to it that the name Petty was listed as a NASCAR winner. The linking of the name "Petty" with victory would be repeated hundreds of times over the years.

In 1954, Lee Petty claimed the NASCAR Grand National championship, having already driven to nearly twenty wins in just six seasons. He repeated as NASCAR champion in both 1958 and 1959, winning eleven races in the latter season.

One of those victories came in yet another historic NASCAR race. Big Bill France had long dreamed of building a racetrack unlike any other. Against the odds, he completed Daytona International Speedway—the most famous of all NASCAR superspeedways—in time for the track to host the first Daytona 500 in February 1959. To help make his new venture a success, France needed a race that would have people talking. As things turned out, he needn't have worried.

Lee Petty had qualified his 1959 Oldsmobile in the fifteenth starting position, and once the green flag waved he began to work his way toward the front of the pack. On lap 150, Petty moved into the lead for the first time, taking the position from Johnny Beauchamp. From that point on, the two drivers swapped the top spot back and forth in a thrilling battle that had the 40,000 spectators on their feet. But the real excitement was yet to come.

On the last lap of the race, as the lead cars powered out of the final turn and headed toward the finish line, Petty's Olds pulled alongside leader Beauchamp's T-Bird. They crossed the line in a dead heat. NASCAR officials sent Beauchamp to victory lane, but Petty immediately lodged a protest. France declared the results unofficial, and set about reviewing the evidence. Finally, three days later, photography and films proved that Lee Petty had been right all along. He was pronounced champion of that first, unforgettable Daytona 500.

Another member of the Petty family also competed in that memorable race, although with dramatically less success. Finishing fifty-seventh out of fifty-nine drivers was Richard Petty, Lee's son, driving in the Convertible division.

The previous year Richard had made his first Grand National starts, including one that looked to be his first victory—until the win was taken away after a postrace scoring protest by another driver.

ABOVE: Kyle Petty's greatest Winston Cup Series success came in the 1990s, when he drove the unmistakable black-and-green Pontiacs fielded by Felix Sabates. Kyle left the Sabates team after the 1996 season, having won six races since their partnership began in 1990.

OPPOSITE TOP: Kyle Petty differs from his father in many ways, but he has always been a popular driver among both the fans and the media. When asked a question, Kyle's reply is thorough and thoughtful, making him an important spokesman for stock car racing.

The driver who had initiated the protest? Richard's father, Lee. No matter, though, for Richard Petty was bound for glory.

Richard Petty was awarded Rookie of the Year honors in 1959 and became a NASCAR Grand National winner in 1960, after driving to victory at North Carolina's Charlotte Fairgrounds dirt track in his family's Plymouth. That was to be the first of 200 victories, a NASCAR wins total that will never be matched.

Though father and son raced against each other several times as Richard's career got underway, the familial battles came to an end in 1961 at Daytona International Speedway. In the first qualifying race leading up to the Daytona 500, Richard Petty was injured in a crash that occurred when Junior Johnson's car got tangled up with Petty's Plymouth. In the second qualifying race, Lee Petty met greater disaster. Both Lee and his rival from the first Daytona 500, Johnny Beauchamp, were involved in a crash, climbed the guardrail, and were catapulted out of the track. Lee Petty suffered many broken bones and extensive internal injuries. For all practical purposes, his NASCAR career ended that day.

Richard, though, continued to represent the family in victory lane after victory lane, with many of his wins coming in cars prepared by his brother, Maurice, a brilliant mechanic. "Petty blue" became a color recognized by stock car fans around the world, and Richard himself became known as "King Richard."

Not that Richard had anything to do with bestowing himself such a title: Petty was always humble, ready to meet with his fans, and willing to talk to the media. Instead, King Richard was anointed by those who were in understandable awe of what Petty was accomplishing on the speedways. By the time he retired from racing in 1992, Petty had seven NASCAR championships to go with his astonishing wins total, including twenty-seven victories in 1967 alone. His career winning average of victories versus starts is 17 percent, and he claimed an impressive 126 pole positions.

When Richard climbed from his Winston Cup car after his final ride at Atlanta Motor Speedway in 1992, the Petty name still drove on. Richard's son, Kyle, had shown flashes of family brilliance in winning the first race he ever ran at Daytona International Speedway, in an Auto Racing Club of America (ARCA) competition in 1979. Later that year, Kyle began to join his father in Winston Cup competition.

Through the 2000 season, Kyle Petty had scored eight Winston Cup wins, two with the famed Wood Brothers team and six during a lengthy association with car owner Felix Sabates. But as the years passed, Kyle began to look forward to passing the torch to his own son, young Adam Petty, the fourth generation of the racing Pettys.

Adam also had inherited the family's talent for motorsports excellence, winning in ARCA and American Speed Association (ASA) competition. The long-range goal was for Adam to compete in NASCAR's Busch Series, and then move up to Winston Cup in his Petty Enterprises entry. Sadly, it was not to be, for Adam was killed in his Busch car while practicing at New Hampshire International Speedway in April 2000.

ABOVE: The death of Adam Petty in 2000 tested Kyle in ways most people can never imagine. For any father to lose his son is a tragedy, but the constant media pressure that accompanies the high-profile sport of stock car racing made life even more difficult after Adam's death.

Later that season, Kyle Petty took over the wheel and drove for his son's Petty Enterprises team, finishing his Busch Series commitment. In 2001, the team Adam Petty had been destined to drive for made the move to NASCAR's elite division, with father Kyle in the driver's seat.

THE
Jarrett
family

"**D**ale Jarrett's going to win the Daytona 500!" Those excited words, carried across the airwaves to a CBS television audience of millions, held special significance for the man speaking them. It was February 14, 1993, and the broadcaster calling the finish of NASCAR's greatest race, the Daytona 500, was Ned Jarrett, whose own son was streaking across the finish line in triumph.

The story of the Jarrett family and their success in stock car racing began nearly forty years before that sunny afternoon in 1993.

In 1953, a young man from the Conover, North Carolina, area first dared to compete in NASCAR's burgeoning Grand National series. That driver was Ned Jarrett.

Born on October 12, 1932, Ned grew up in a family of farmers who also operated a sawmill near Conover. His natural interest in machinery was heightened by the opening of the now-legendary Hickory Speedway, a small racetrack that would bring fierce dirt-track competition to the region.

Jarrett competed at the first race held at Hickory, driving a battered race car he had won in a poker game. A respectable tenth-place finish planted a seed of stock car driving ambition in the young man's mind, though family pressures caused Ned to temporarily vacate the driver's seat.

But the lure of racing was too strong, and soon Ned—with his family's approval—was building a name for himself in the racing world. He had set

his sights on the NASCAR Grand National Series, the elite division of the swiftly growing motor-sports sanctioning body.

Sporadic Grand National starts in the years 1953 to 1958 yielded little success, but Ned was unwaveringly persistent, his family having taught him the importance of determination in achieving goals.

In 1959, Jarrett raced his way to victory lane twice, in seventeen starts. Jarrett took forty green flags in 1960—and increased his win tally to five. His fellow competitors—such legends of stock car racing as Lee and Richard Petty, Joe Weatherly, Ralph Earnhardt, Rex White, and Tom Pistone—had no choice but to appreciate the talents of the young driver who had made such an impact on the division's tough competition.

In particular, the rivalry between Jarrett and the famed Junior Johnson was heated. Johnson was an ex-bootlegger, a driver whose fearless aggression and rough-and-tumble style caused other drivers to give him plenty of leeway on the track. But Jarrett stood his ground on the speedways, and the automotive combat between the two NASCAR greats became the stuff of legends. So intense and fearsome was the rivalry that NASCAR founder Bill France felt the need to summon the two drivers into

PREVIOUS PAGES: In 1964, Ned Jarrett often had to look to the rear to spot his competition. The popular driver won fifteen races that season, more than any other competitor. THIS PAGE: In 1965, Ned Jarrett won thirteen races and the NASCAR championship, making incidents like this spin at Charlotte Motor Speedway a rarity during such a sterling season.

his presence for a reality check before the situation got out of control.

Fortunately for Jarrett, the feuding with Johnson had little effect on the young driver's success, and in 1961 Ned Jarrett won his first Grand National championship. In 1964, Jarrett won fourteen races driving for the Ford factory–supported car owned by Bondy Long. And in 1965, Jarrett won a second series title in a season that featured thirteen wins.

In contrast to Junior Johnson's daring charges, Ned's on-track style was more determined. Intelligence played as great a part as risk-taking when Ned took to the track, and his calm demeanor earned him the nickname "Gentleman Ned."

At the age of thirty-four, Ned Jarrett retired from racing. The decision shocked the Grand National world. Here was a driver who seemed to have it all—a strong Ford ride, a proven track record, and two series titles. But Jarrett had other things that mattered to him—a son, Glenn, already in high school, a young daughter, Patti, and a second son, ten-year-old Dale. Jarrett had seen Fireball

Roberts killed, and knew his own wife, Martha, would be relieved if Ned ended his racing career.

Fittingly, Ned became manager of Hickory Speedway, the very same North Carolina track where his racing career had begun. But greater things were in store yet for the fearless, gentlemanly ex-driver. Ned took a Dale Carnegie course to improve his public speaking abilities, the first step on a new journey that would eventually make him one of America's most beloved motorsports broadcasters.

Meanwhile, young Dale Jarrett, born November 26, 1956, had inherited his father's love for racing. It was almost inevitable—after all, Dale grew up playing in the infields of racetracks with the sons of the men his father raced against, week-in and week-out.

Though tempted by his (considerable) skill at golf to follow a much quieter sports career pursuit, in his early twenties Dale was lured away from the links by the siren's call of a NASCAR career. "I wanted to race for a living," Dale recalled of his early racing days. "I had become a scratch golfer and had thought seriously about trying to make a career of golf. I received a lot of encouragement from

For years NASCAR drivers had dreamed of racing at historic Indianapolis Motor Speedway, and in 1994, the dream came true with the inauguration of the annual Brickyard 400. To date, Dale Jarrett has won the prestigious event twice.

my parents about golf. Dad knew the hardships and pitfalls of racing and he didn't want me to go through them. My mother had worried about dad racing for years and she didn't want another one in the family to worry over.

"But there was no doubt in my mind about what I wanted to do. After dad saw that I was serious about racing, he gave me his full support, as he would have done regardless of what I had chosen to do."

Racing in the newly christened Busch Grand National Series in 1982, Dale impressed the NASCAR world with a sixth-place finish in the points standings, and the future champion claimed top-ten finishes in more than half the races in which he competed. A Grand National win finally came in 1986, but Dale had already set his sights on the elite NASCAR division, the Winston Cup Series.

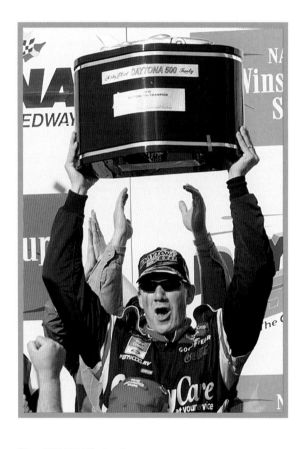

Many NASCAR Winston Cup drivers consider victory in the Daytona 500 to be the pinnacle of a driving career. Dale Jarrett has scaled that pinnacle several times during his career, scoring coveted wins in 1993, 1996, and 2000.

His first start in Winston Cup racing came in 1984, but trying to break into the series with a handful of appearances was a frustrating experience. Still, Dale made the most of the opportunities he was given, and people were noticing that he finished well when he had the chance to race at the Winston Cup level.

Among those who had noticed Jarrett's talent was Virginia's famous racing clan, the Wood Brothers. When the Woods' driver, Neil Bonnett, was hurt early in the 1990 season, Eddie Wood knew Dale Jarrett was the man to call. Days later, Jarrett was behind the wheel of the Wood Brothers' red and white Ford Thunderbird. At last, Jarrett had his full-time Winston Cup ride.

Dale Jarrett drove to seven top-tens in that first season, and had performed well into 1991. When the Winston Cup Series arrived at Michigan International Speedway for the race held on August 18, people were saying it was time for Dale to win. He did just that, battling door-to-door with Davey Allison as the two Thunderbirds powered toward the checkered flag. Jarrett nosed ahead by inches at the finish line, finally tasting triumph. The victory was made even sweeter by the fact that Ned Jarrett was calling the race for ESPN's television broadcast.

With consistent strong finishes and a win under his belt, Dale Jarrett was a hot commodity in stock car racing. And when National Football League coach Joe Gibbs decided to start his own Winston Cup team for 1992, Dale got the call.

Not surprisingly, the Gibbs team went winless in its first season, as new teams often do. But they struck gold immediately in 1993. On the last lap of the Daytona 500, Jarrett's bright green Chevrolet led off the final turn, with Dale Earnhardt's fearsome black Lumina inches behind. High above the track, Ned Jarrett provided the commentary from the CBS television booth as son Dale won the Daytona 500, an emotional victory for the Jarrett family.

In 1995, Jarrett took up an offer to move to the highly regarded Ford team of Robert Yates Racing after driver Ernie Irvan was injured. The Yates-Jarrett alliance was to become one that would add volumes to the NASCAR record books.

In 1996, driving a new number 88 car and supported by a crew led by Todd Parrott, Dale Jarrett claimed his second Daytona 500. Later in the season, Jarrett won the third annual Brickyard 400 at Indianapolis Motor Speedway. In 1997, the team won seven times, and then added three more victories in 1998.

Consistently at the top of the Winston Cup points standings year after year, Jarrett's team put all the pieces together in 1999. The year's hard fought battles amounted to four wins, six second-places, four third-places, five fourth-places, and five fifth-places giving Dale Jarrett and his team the Winston Cup championship.

Taken together, the records of father Ned and son Dale are packed with championship-caliber statistics and tales of victory in NASCAR's greatest races. And, as Dale proved when he won a third Daytona 500 in 2000, the tale of the Jarrett family still has many chapters yet to be written.

Winning pole position in the March 2001 Cracker Barrel 500 as well as starring in a series of humorous television commercials for his new sponsor, United Parcel Service, reinforced Dale Jarrett's marketability.

THE
Marlin
Family

W hile the North Carolina region became ground zero for the formation of NASCAR's early touring itinerary, competitors aiming to run in the Grand National Series came from throughout the South. Among the drivers drawn to NASCAR's top division was a man from Tennessee, nicknamed Coo Coo. And though he would never win in fifteen years of Grand National competition, the passion for the sport of stock car racing that he passed on to his son would begin a chain of events leading to the family's name being engraved on the trophy that symbolizes victory in NASCAR's greatest race.

Clifton Marlin, known as Coo Coo, hailed from Columbia, Tennessee, and first took on the Grand National Series in 1966 with a single start that nonetheless yielded a top-ten finish. Though Coo Coo was an experienced short-track racer, the move to NASCAR's top division proved to be daunting (as it does for many young racers). But by the time the series had been renamed the Winston Cup Series, Coo Coo had built up a valuable store of stock car racing experience and was prepared to take on the challenges ahead of him.

When the Winston Cup Series arrived at Texas World Speedway for its June 25, 1972 race at the two-mile (3.2km) superspeedway near the town of College Station, the best Marlin could do in qualifying his Chevrolet was a twenty-first-place starting position. But on a blisteringly hot summer day, Marlin passed car after car, falling just short in his quest to win. Still, a third-place finish was more than respectable considering that the drivers who finished ahead of Marlin were Bobby Allison and race winner Richard Petty.

Just more than a year later, Marlin again took home a third-place finish, this time at his home track, Fairgrounds Speedway in Nashville. And on May 10, 1975, Marlin was third again at Nashville. These three races were the popular driver's best finishes.

Interestingly, the second of Marlin's Nashville top-threes came in a race that was Darrell Waltrip's first Winston Cup victory. Waltrip had cut his teeth in Sportsman races on the half-mile (0.8km) speedway in Nashville, which was exactly what another young driver—Coo Coo's son, Sterling—was doing at the time.

Sterling had grown up around racing, so it was almost inevitable that the young man would try his hand at his father's profession. And when Coo Coo suffered a broken shoulder before the Nashville Winston Cup race on May 8, 1976, the veteran driver didn't go far to get a replacement. Eighteen-year-old Sterling made his first Winston Cup start at his home track. Though Sterling started dead last in the thirty-car field and finished twenty-ninth after an oil pump failure sent him to the garage, it was just the beginning of a long and fruitful career.

Not that success came to Coo Coo's son immediately: Sterling ran for a variety of car owners throughout the 1980s, not scoring even a top-five until 1986.

Still, Sterling's performances attracted the eye of car owner Billy Hagan, who'd won the Winston Cup championship in 1984 with driver Terry Labonte. Hagan signed Marlin in 1987, and for the next four years Marlin edged closer and closer to the elusive first win. Indeed, counting two years driving for Junior Johnson and one with the Stavola Brothers after leaving Hagan, Marlin had finished as run-ner-up in Winston Cup races a frustrating eight times by the end of 1993. But Sterling's perseverance and desire to win was unbeatable.

For 1994, Sterling signed with the venerable Morgan-McClure team of Virginia. Teamed with crew chief Tony Glover and engine builder Runt Pittman, Marlin started the season positive he could finally win a Winston Cup race. It didn't take long. Marlin qualified fourth for the Daytona 500, and ran up front all day long. As the laps wound down Marlin was in front, and with determination he held off a charge from Ernie Irvan to claim his first victory. A proud Coo Coo joined his son in victory lane to celebrate the Marlin family's victory in "The Great American Race."

Sterling went on to repeat as Daytona 500 winner in 1995, and claimed superspeedway wins in 1996 at the 400-mile (640km) Daytona summer race and at Alabama's Talladega Superspeedway.

A favorite family memory of Sterling's has to do with Talladega, when Coo Coo had to break the news to his wife that young Sterling would be racing on NASCAR's fastest superspeedway. The elder Marlin chose dinner as the appropriate time to make his announcement, but couldn't find a good way to bring up the topic.

"He was spearing a piece of meat," Sterling recalled, "and looking away from her and he said, 'Pass them potatoes there, Eula Faye. Sterling's running at Talladega.'"

THE
Allison *Family*

The Alabama Gang. Say those three little words to any longtime race fan, and he or she will probably begin recounting favorite chapters from one of the great stories of stock car racing, a story that began when two brothers moved from Florida to Alabama to pursue their dream of making a living by racing cars. Their dream came true, but in the end they got much more than they'd bargained for; and like any epic, the story of the Allisons ranges over considerable emotional ground, from incredible triumph to devastating tragedy.

The Allison saga begins with brothers Bobby and Donnie (born on December 3, 1937, and September 7, 1939, respectively), Florida short-track racers who migrated to Alabama in search of greener racing pastures. They became legendary short-track competitors throughout the South, each of the drivers gaining a reputation as a fearsome competitor.

Bobby first raced in NASCAR's top division in 1961, and followed a handful of starts with a full-time entry in NASCAR racing in 1966, the same year Donnie made his first start. Bobby raced to three wins in that first season, and finished tenth in the championship points standings. He raced on to the 1983 Winston Cup championship, and won the Daytona 500 in 1978 and 1982.

Donnie, after making his own move into full-time Winston Cup competition, found his own success, winning ten races between 1966 and 1988.

In 1988, Bobby Allison was determined to win his third Daytona 500, but late in the race he faced a stiff challenge from a young Alabama driver at the wheel of a Ford—Bobby's own son, Davey, who had begun his own Winston Cup career three years earlier. The father and son swept to a one-two finish in the great race.

Later that season, Bobby crashed hard at Pennsylvania's Pocono International Raceway, and the resulting head injuries ended the great driver's career.

Meanwhile, son Davey raced on, quickly establishing himself as one of Winston Cup racing's super-stars. After winning numerous races at the dawn of the 1990s, Davey joined his father as a Daytona 500 winner after a superb performance at the legendary Florida superspeedway in 1992. Davey nearly won the 1992 Winston Cup championship, falling just short when he crashed (through no fault of his own) late in the final race of the season.

Davey's future was bright, and he was expected to continue his meteoric career. But in July 1993, while landing a helicopter at Alabama's Talladega Superspeedway, Davey Allison was killed when the air-craft crashed into the ground. Davey's death came just more than a year after the death of his younger brother Clifford, killed at Michigan International Speedway while practicing for a NASCAR Busch Series race. The family was devastated.

Although nothing can bring back Davey Allison or console family, friends, and fans, his legend lives on. Davey Allison has been inducted into three halls of fame: the National Motorsports Press Association's Stock Car Hall of Fame at Darlington Raceway (in 1996), Bristol Motor Speedway's Heroes of Bristol Hall of Fall (in 1997), and the International Motorsports Hall of Fame in Talladega (in 1998).

The story of the racing Allisons is one that should still be in the process of being written. That it came to such a premature conclusion is one of the great tragedies of the sport.

PREVIOUS PAGES: Bobby Allison (center) enjoys the thrills of victory lane after winning the 1988 Daytona 500 in his Buick, having edged out his son Davey for the win. OPPOSITE PAGE, TOP: Donnie Allison brought his talents to America's most famous race, the Indianapolis 500. Pictured here in 1971 with the legendary A.J. Foyt (left), Donnie enjoys a break during qualifying for the Memorial Day classic. OPPOSITE PAGE, BOTTOM: Though he would eventually fall out of the race with engine failure, Bobby Allison here leads the front pack in the 1976 Daytona 500. Close behind are (left to right) David Pearson, Richard Petty, and A.J. Foyt. THIS PAGE: Bobby Allison is pictured with a 1973 Chevrolet, one of the cars from the race team he owned.

OPPOSITE PAGE: Donnie Allison's car is in for service in the midst of the 1974 Daytona 500. Trading the lead with brother Bobby several times, Donnie eventually finished in sixth place.

THIS PAGE, TOP: A worried Davey Allison in the 28 car passes the scene of father Bobby's crash at Pocono International Raceway on June 19, 1988. Bobby's severe injuries led to his retirement from racing.

THIS PAGE, BOTTOM: Davey Allison prepares to race in 1992. The young driver's good looks and hard charges on the track made him tremendously popular with race fans.

I t's true that to the casual race fan, the driver is the guy who deserves all the praise when he makes his way to victory lane. But anyone who bothers to take even the most cursory of glances behind the scenes will soon see that it is the race team as a whole that enables the drivers to race to greater glory. In NASCAR, there are race teams whose history isn't measured just in years, but in decades. Such is the case with Virginia's Wood Brothers race team, an operation that was there in the beginning and still races on in the new millennium of NASCAR competition.

NASCAR's very first Strictly Stock race had been held just four years earlier when a young driver from Stuart, Virginia, named Glen Wood made his first start. Already an experienced Modified driver, it took Wood five years of sporadic runs, until 1957, before he won his first Grand National top-ten; then over the next two seasons he improved and scored runner-up finishes.

By 1960, it was clear that Wood was a contender. And when he did win, he did it in a big way. On April 18, 1960, Glen Wood qualified on the pole and then led all 200 laps to easily beat Rex White, Jimmy Massey, and Richard Petty at Bowman Gray Stadium in Winston-Salem, North Carolina. Wood repeated the feat on the same track twice more that season.

Throughout his driving career, Glen was joined by his brother Leonard and other family members in car preparation. The two brothers gave their operation a simple name, the Wood Brothers. And despite Glen's talent behind the wheel, he and Leonard slowly began to focus increasingly on providing exceptionally prepared stock cars for other drivers. Following Glen's last Grand National start in 1964,

OPPOSITE PAGE: The Wood Brothers pit crew prepares to spring into action at Darlington Raceway in 1977. The team is credited with discovering new methods of pitting stock cars, ushering in the era of today's fourteen-second pit stops.
THIS PAGE: Leonard Wood prepares the team's Ford at Bristol Motor Speedway. After several winless years, driver Elliott Sadler brought the Woods back to victory lane with his 2001 Bristol win.

an incredible roster of talent began to compete for the Wood Brothers Ford teams. Glen Wood's gift with race cars, both behind the wheel and under the hood, was great.

Indeed, the Woods had proven how competitive their cars could be in the running of the 1963 Daytona 500. The brothers had enlisted proven race-winning driver Marvin Panch to compete in the important event, but trouble struck the team when Panch was injured in a testing-session crash. Fellow driver Tiny Lund ran to Panch's aid, helping to extricate Marvin from the flaming wreckage.

From his hospital bed, Panch asked Glen and Leonard to allow Lund to wheel the Wood Brothers entry for him in the big race. The Woods agreed, and their faith was rewarded when Lund took the lead with eight laps remaining. Lund held off Fred Lorenzen and Ned Jarrett to bring victory to the Wood Brothers race team, their first of four Daytona 500 wins.

Glen's sons Len and Eddie joined on in the early 1970s, helping to elevate the Wood Brothers team to new heights in the Winston Cup Series. Much of the team's glory came in the years 1972 to 1979, when the great "Silver Fox," David Pearson, raced for the Wood Brothers and crossed the finish line first an incredible forty-three times in 143 starts.

Perhaps Pearson's greatest victory for the Wood Brothers was in the 1976 Daytona 500, when he and Richard Petty clashed coming off the final turn as the two legends roared toward the checkered flag. Both Pearson's Mercury and Petty's Dodge collided and spun, but despite the chaos, Pearson managed to keep his engine running. Slipping the car into gear, Pearson limped across the finish line and gave the Wood Brothers their fourth win in NASCAR's greatest race.

In recent years, the Wood Brothers have had success with such drivers as Dale Jarrett and Morgan Shepherd, and began an association with talented young Virginia driver Elliott Sadler in 1999.

Sadler struggled as he learned in the Winston Cup Series, and some observers felt that the Wood Brothers' single-car-entry team had allowed time and progress to pass them by. But the Woods reorganized their team after the 2001 season, and entered the new season with renewed confidence.

The Winston Cup world soon found that confidence was justified. On March 25, 2001, Elliott Sadler held off the charge of John Andretti and returned the Wood Brothers to a Winston Cup Series victory lane for the first time since 1993. The victory at Tennessee's Bristol Motor Speedway was Sadler's first; for the Wood Brothers, it was number ninety-seven.

With a resurgent spirit and a new sense of competitiveness, the efforts of Virginia's Wood Brothers will continue to be a crucial part of NASCAR racing.

GM
Goodwrench Service Plus
Goodwrench Service Plus
BURGER KING
Snap-on
GOODYEAR
76
RCR
GM
Goodwrench Service Plus
NASCAR
Winston Cup
7 Time Champion
Coca-Cola
Team REALTREE
ACDelco
GM
Goodwrench Service Plus

Earnhardt *family*

There are tangible items that can help sum up a career spent in stock car racing. There are statistics that total up victories, numbers that point out how many pole positions were won, how many top-fives were racked up, how many laps were led. And then there are the intangibles. Things that can't be measured by facts and figures. Things like toughness. Determination. Aggression. And the pure will to win. Those are the elements that create legends, and in stock car racing there is one family whose story has all of those qualities in abundance—the Earnhardt family.

Ralph Earnhardt

The story begins with a man who was one of the toughest ever to wheel a stock car around a dirt track in NASCAR's formative years. It continued with his son, who became arguably the greatest natural talent ever to compete in NASCAR's elite division. And it continues today with the grandson, as the newest generation begins to live up to the imposing standards set by his predecessors. If any family's tradition proudly represents all that is good about NASCAR, it is the Earnhardts'.

Ralph Earnhardt built a reputation—a deserved reputation—for being one of the toughest stock car drivers around. No less an expert than Bobby Isaac, NASCAR's 1970 champion, called Ralph "one of the best short-track drivers ever." And two-time NASCAR champion Ned Jarrett summed up Earnhardt as "the most intense, hard-driven man I have ever known."

OPPOSITE PAGE: To many diehard fans of the sport—and to even more people who know little about stock car racing—this image epitomized NASCAR's Winston Cup Series. Along with Richard Petty, Dale Earnhardt defined his era.
THIS PAGE: In July 1961, Ralph Earnhardt drove for famed car owner Cotton Owens in the Firecracker 250 NASCAR Grand National race at Daytona International Speedway. Ralph claimed a top-ten finish.

In an eight-year period beginning in 1956, Ralph Earnhardt started in just more than fifty Grand National events, and he never made his way to victory lane, although he twice finished in second. But it wasn't so much his record that sums up his efforts as it is the memories of the drivers who had to battle against him on the racetrack.

Doubtless, Earnhardt could have left more impressive statistics in his wake had he competed in the top division of NASCAR more frequently. But Ralph did not like the travel demanded by the growing series, which often saw more than fifty races held from sea to sea each season. Instead, Ralph concentrated on supporting his family by racing—and winning—on North Carolina short tracks like Hickory Speedway and Concord Speedway, tracks that were close to his home in Kannapolis, North Carolina.

Ralph's bare-bones racing efforts were occasionally augmented with the help of a young man with

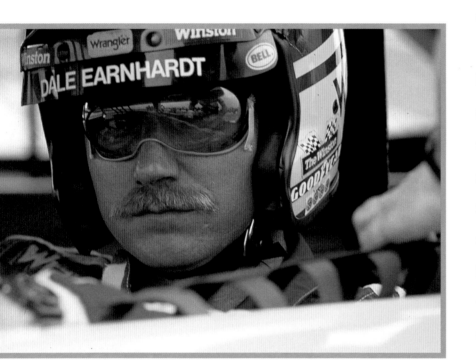

Dale Earnhardt's game face—the look that gave rise to his nickname "The Intimidator." Of course, the amazing on-track moves that Earnhardt pulled from his bag of tricks only served to give new meaning to the name.

an intense expression, Ralph's son Dale.

Racing was in Dale Earnhardt's blood, and he grew up fascinated by his father's exploits and the race car that was ever present on the family's modest property. Young Dale quit school in 1966 at the age of sixteen, determined to make his way in racing. Though father Ralph was furious at his son's decision, he began to respect his son's determination to succeed behind the wheel of a stock car while holding down jobs at a service station and a mill.

Dale had begun to succeed at racing when he was struck by a devastating blow—Ralph Earnhardt collapsed and died while working in his car on September 27, 1973.

The loss of his father fueled young Dale's determination to make it, and in May 1975, Earnhardt parlayed his growing reputation as a talented driver to earn a start in his first Winston Cup race. Running in the 600-mile (960km) event at Charlotte Motor Speedway, Earnhardt bettered his starting position by eleven spots and came home in twenty-second place. It was only the beginning.

By 1979, Earnhardt had been chosen for a full-time position behind the wheel of Rod Osterlund's Chevrolet. On April 1, 1979, at Tennessee's treacherous Bristol International Raceway, in just his sixteenth Winston Cup start, Dale Earnhardt beat Bobby Allison and all of NASCAR's stars. It was to be the first of seventy-six career victories in NASCAR's Winston Cup Series.

In 1980, Earnhardt proved that he was the real deal. NASCAR legend Cale Yarborough was determined to win the season championship—the only problem was that the points lead was held by 1979 Rookie of the Year Dale Earnhardt. Yarborough had closed to within twenty-nine points as the NASCAR stock cars arrived for the season finale at California's Ontario Motor Speedway. Earnhardt overcame obstacles in the race that would have set back many long-time stock car veterans on his way to finishing in fifth place, good enough to bring him one of the two most significant accomplishments of stock car racing, the Winston Cup Series championship. That honor would be his six more times in his lifetime.

There is one other tremendous goal that every driver dreams of: winning the Daytona 500. After aligning himself in a partnership with former-racer-turned-car-owner Richard Childress, Earnhardt climbed to the top of his sport. He won race after race, championship after championship. But one title proved elusive time after time. He just couldn't win the Daytona 500.

In 1998, as was the case so many other years before, Dale Earnhardt looked to be a top contender in the great race as the green flag of the Daytona 500 neared. And after the race began, his black Chevrolet soon made its way to the front of the field. But that had been the case many times before,

Both Davey Allison in number 28 and Dale Earnhardt in number 3 enjoyed running in the NASCAR Busch Grand National Series as well as the Winston Cup Series. Regardless of where they raced—pictured here in 1989 at Nazareth Speedway—the fierce competition between the two great drivers was always intense.

when fate had always sent Earnhardt home with victory in the Daytona 500 just out of reach. Dale was determined to enjoy a different outcome this year.

It was a battle of speed and aerodynamics and pure courage, and Earnhardt was a master of all three. As the end of the race grew close he fended off charge after charge from his fellow competitors, each of them equally determined to win NASCAR's greatest race. But this year, at last, they were the ones who headed home in defeat. Dale Earnhardt won the Daytona 500. And in a measure of the respect Earnhardt had earned in his career, all of the crew members of the other teams lined pit road at Daytona International Speedway to demonstrate their appreciation for Dale's accomplishment.

On February 18, 2001, Dale Earnhardt was once again a contender for victory in the Daytona 500. But perhaps even more important, Earnhardt was a contender for a NASCAR-record eighth championship. In the year 2000, Earnhardt had just missed the title in a season-long battle with Bobby Labonte. Now, with the 2001 season at hand, Dale knew a good finish in the Daytona 500 could help provide a foundation for capturing the championship.

On the last turn of the final lap of the Daytona 500, Dale was running in third place, but he was pressured by a large group of cars that created an aerodynamic disturbance. In the battle for position

BELOW LEFT: Dale Earnhardt (center) poses proudly with his two sons, Dale Jr. (left) and Kerry (right) just before all three competed at Michigan International Speedway on August 20, 2000, in the Pepsi 400. BELOW RIGHT: As Michael Waltrip drove his Dale Earnhardt Incorporated Chevrolet to the win, with Dale Jr. close behind, this terrible crash that took the life of Dale Earnhardt unfolded just behind them.

at speeds close to 200 miles per hour (320kph), Earnhardt's car lost control and climbed the banking of the track, striking the retaining wall. Dale Earnhardt was killed on impact, and the sport of stock car racing suffered a devastating blow.

As terrible a blow as the loss of NASCAR's biggest superstar was to the racing professionals and to the fans, it was far worse for the driver who finished second in the 2001 Daytona 500, Dale Earnhardt Jr.

The third-generation Earnhardt driver had made his first Winston Cup starts in 1999, competing in five races while maintaining his focus on the Busch Grand National Series. But after becoming the 1999 Busch Series champion—the second year in a row he won the title—Dale Jr. was ready to make the Winston Cup move.

In just the seventh race of the 2000 season, Dale Earnhardt Jr. drove to his first Winston Cup Series victory, holding off his father and the other stars of NASCAR at Texas Motor Speedway. Dale Jr. also won later in the season at Richmond International Raceway, and was fastest qualifier at two other events in the season.

On August 20, 2000, at Michigan Speedway, Dale Earnhardt had become only the second father ever to compete against two sons in a NASCAR event, when Kerry Earnhardt joined his father and Dale Jr. in Winston Cup racing. Only Lee Petty had ever raced against two sons, when the elder Petty competed against Richard and Maurice.

As is the case with the Petty name, the Earnhardt name embodies stock car racing. And with Kerry Earnhardt showing his talent and Dale Jr. an established Winston Cup superstar, the link between NASCAR and Earnhardt could easily stand for decades—and generations—to come.

In honor of Ralph Earnhardt, Dale Jr. uses the number 8, which was his grandfather's racing number. With a passion for motorsports running deep in his bloodlines, Dale Jr. perseveres here at Bristol in March 2001—his first race after his father's death.

THE
Waltrip
Family

D arrell Waltrip knew he was good at stock car racing and had a lot to say about the sport and those who competed in it—and he never hesitated to speak his mind. Waltrip's propensity for holding nothing back earned him a dubious nickname ("Jaws"), along with the love of some fans and the enmity of as many others. But by the time he retired, Darrell climbed from the cockpit with the universal respect of the NASCAR Winston Cup community.

The young driver from Kentucky had cut his teeth on the short track in Nashville, Tennessee, and made his first Winston Cup start in 1972 driving a self-owned stock car. Darrell started twenty-fifth and finished thirty-eighth after engine problems sidelined him. It wasn't the most successful of debuts, but big things were on the horizon.

In 1975, Waltrip's first Winston Cup win came, and over his twenty-nine-year career Darrell would score eighty-three more victories. After a successful alliance with car owner Bill Gardner, Waltrip signed up with Junior Johnson in 1981, winning back-to-back NASCAR Winston Cup championships. Waltrip, armed with on-track success, wasn't hesitant to spread his candid point of view off the track, earning the nickname "Jaws" from his fellow competitors.

But regardless of the nickname, Darrell continued to set a blazing pace in NASCAR racing, winning his third championship with Johnson in 1985. He began a four-year association with car owner Rick Hendrick in 1987, a stint that was highlighted by a victory in the 1989 Daytona 500.

In the later years of Darrell's great career, he encountered a number of unexpected obstacles. Following the successful course of the late Alan Kulwicki, who won the NASCAR Winston Cup championship in 1992 while driving for a race team that he owned himself, Darrell Waltrip joined several other drivers in attempting to become both a successful owner and driver.

OPPOSITE PAGE, TOP: Young
Darrell Waltrip poses before
the 1973 Daytona 500. He
would finish twelfth in that
race, with his quest to win
NASCAR's greatest race
remaining a futile one until
1989.
OPPOSITE PAGE, BOTTOM:
Darrell joined several of his
fellow drivers in a trend
toward owning their own
teams. But like the majority of
the other owner-drivers,
Waltrip found the business
demands of running a
Winston Cup operation to be a
distraction from his on-track
charges.

At first, it looked as though making the ownership leap would pay Waltrip benefits. In 1991 he won two races, and three more in 1992. But those would be the final wins of his career, as the pressures of both administering a race team and driving for it began to slowly wear on Darrell and the operation.

Though he often joked in television interviews by adopting dual personalities of the yokel driver and the business-conscious owner, the challenges confronting Waltrip were no laughing matter. The performance of his team began a noticeable decline, with his entry sinking to twenty-ninth in the 1996 championship standings. Finally, in 1998, Waltrip was forced to admit that his owner/driver experiment had been a failure.

An ugly episode involving a botched team merger and sponsorship package with Tabasco further hurt Waltrip's on-track performances. But just when the light of Waltrip's career had dimmed almost totally, an unexpected opportunity for competitive redemption was presented.

Early in the 1998 season, the talented young driver Steve Park was injured in a serious crash. Dale Earnhardt had chosen Park to drive for the new race team he owned, and with Park out of action, Dale needed a substitute behind the wheel. Earnhardt turned to Waltrip.

Given the opportunity to once again drive a competitive car in the elite series, Waltrip responded with enthusiasm. He soon drove the car to a top-five finish, and reawakened the respect of the Winston Cup world.

Waltrip's time driving for Earnhardt was short-term, though, and Darrell finished his career on a "Victory Tour" in 2000 that offered little chance of victory. Since then, Darrell Waltrip has made a rapid transition to the world of motorsports broadcasting, where he offers a combination of the unique competitive perspective of a Winston Cup champion and the outspoken demeanor of a man unafraid to say exactly what he means.

Darrell's younger brother Michael faced his greatest travails during the first fifteen years of his Winston Cup career, mainly in the form of a question that didn't go away until February 18, 2001. That question was, "Will Michael Waltrip ever win a NASCAR Winston Cup points race?"

He had come close. In 1988, 1990, 1991, 1994, and 1995, Michael had run races where he had come tantalizingly close to earning a trip to victory lane. Each time, circumstances conspired to keep him in second or third place as the checkered flag waved.

Not that there wasn't plenty of evidence that the younger Waltrip had the talent to win in Winston Cup racing. Each year, Charlotte Motor Speedway hosts an R.J. Reynolds–sponsored all-star race for NASCAR's best drivers. During the event in 1996, Michael Waltrip eyed Terry Labonte and

THIS PAGE: Michael Waltrip (left) often turned to brother Darrell (right) for advice. Enduring a winless streak that stretched over hundreds of races, Michael knew it was a lack of top-rate equipment rather than a lack of skill that was keeping him from victory lane.
OPPOSITE PAGE, TOP: The dream of Michael Waltrip comes true at last on February 18, 2001. With Dale Earnhardt Jr. on his rear bumper, Michael Waltrip took the checkered flag in NASCAR Winston Cup competition.
OPPOSITE PAGE, BOTTOM: Joined by his wife, Buffy, Michael and crew are all smiles as they celebrate his win in the 2001 Daytona 500, yet unaware that team owner Dale Earnhardt had met a tragic fate.

Dale Earnhardt battling each other during a late-race restart and bravely shot past both veterans. He drove on to victory in the non-points race.

That win and Michael's ongoing tenacity and belief in himself caught the eye of the great Earnhardt. Dale decided that he wanted to expand the number of cars he would field in 2001 to three. Though Dale himself continued to drive for Richard Childress, Dale Earnhardt Incorporated entered cars for Steve Park and Dale Earnhardt Jr. during the 2000 campaign—and most people expected Earnhardt's Busch Series driver Ron Hornaday would move up to the Winston Cup slot in 2001. So it came as a surprise when Dale announced that his third driver for the 2001 Winston Cup Series would be Michael Waltrip.

Waltrip knew he had the perfect opportunity. Though he'd struggled in the past with inferior cars, now, with Earnhardt's backing, he had the best of equipment and a top-notch crew. But surely Michael also knew that now he almost certainly had to win—no excuses.

If that knowledge placed pressure on Waltrip in the days leading up to the 2001 Daytona 500, it was hard to tell. The driver seemed quietly confident.

When the green flag waved it became clear Waltrip was justifiably confident. He ran at the front of the pack throughout the long day, and as the laps dwindled, he had powered into the lead.

The white flag waved, and the final lap of the Daytona 500 was underway. Waltrip clung to the lead, with Dale Jr. close behind. But both drivers must have been concerned with who was in third—the legendary Dale Earnhardt himself. Having seen Earnhardt charge from deep in the pack to win at Talladega just four months earlier, both Waltrip and Dale Jr. had reason for concern with the black number 3 car just behind.

But fate seemed to favor Waltrip and the younger Earnhardt. As the two cars raced through turns three and four, a larger group of cars in pursuit caught Dale Earnhardt's Chevrolet. As those cars battled for position, Waltrip and Dale Jr. sped away. At last, Michael Waltrip was winning his first points race—and it was happening at the Daytona 500.

Of course, history now offers sad evidence that Waltrip's great victory was overshadowed by the tragic death of Dale Earnhardt, who had crashed in turn four just seconds after Michael roared to victory. But still, fans and competitors alike gained new respect for Michael in the wake of his monumental first victory, and he stands poised to add to the Waltrip legacy.

Parrott *Family*

W hile it is unusual enough that father-and-son drivers have both won NASCAR's most prestigious race, the Daytona 500, it's even more unusual for a crew chief son to join his crew chief father as mastermind behind a victory in "The Great American Race." But in 1998, that's exactly what happened when Todd Parrott, directing the Robert Yates Racing effort with driver Dale Jarrett, matched the feat his father, Buddy, had achieved with driver Derrike Cope eight years earlier.

When Cope took the green flag to begin the 1990 Daytona 500 in a twelfth-place starting position, he was far from a favorite to win the race. Indeed, Dale Earnhardt looked like the driver to beat. Late in the race, Earnhardt's black Chevrolet was the class of the field.

Buddy Parrott, though, had been taking the steps he needed to get his driver in position to win. And when the final caution period began, while the other cars came in for fresh tires, Parrott boldly instructed Cope to remain on the track and gain valuable position. When the green waved for the final time, Earnhardt quickly passed Cope, but Cope remained close to Dale. And when Earnhardt's car suffered a last-lap tire failure, Cope was able to hold off Terry Labonte and Bill Elliott to win NASCAR's biggest race.

"Buddy made the call on the last caution that we were just going to stay out, we were going to go for it," Cope later recalled. It was a call that paid huge dividends.

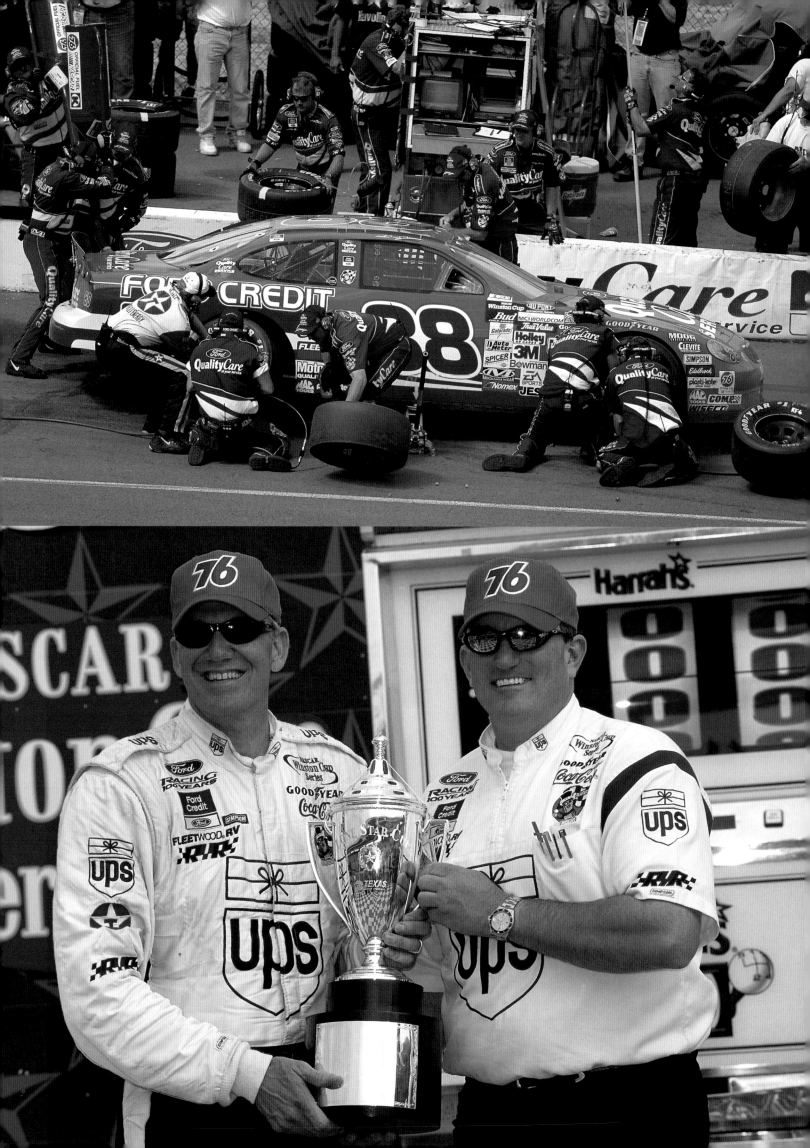

Parrott was confident in making such a call. By the time he was teamed with Cope, he had been involved in racing for more than twenty years, and had been a victorious crew chief with Darrell Waltrip. After leaving Waltrip, Parrott helped guide Richard Petty to victories number 199 and 200, the final two of the King's great career. After winning the Daytona 500 with Cope, Parrott teamed with Rusty Wallace for ten wins in 1993 and eight in 1994, then helped establish Jeff Burton as one of NASCAR's newest stars.

Todd Parrott's first Daytona 500 victory was nearly as improbable as his father's win with Cope had been. Teamed with driver Dale Jarrett, Parrott entered the gates of Daytona International Speedway for the 1996 Daytona 500 as the overseer of a brand new team. Car owner Robert Yates had decided to start a second team operation, and Parrott had been selected to work with Jarrett and the new team based on his seventeen years of experience as a crewman in NASCAR racing.

It's been proven over and over in NASCAR competition that the key to successful teamwork is good chemistry, and that often takes months or even years to develop. But Todd Parrott felt his team had a shot at success, even though Todd had never before played the role of crew chief. He was absolutely right.

After qualifying in third position, Jarrett ran hard all day, and the Daytona 500 came down to a battle between the Dales: Jarrett and Earnhardt. Earnhardt was determined to win, but Jarrett was in front as the final lap began and refused to yield. Dale Jarrett brought home the Daytona 500 trophy in Todd Parrott's debut as a crew chief. This victory was a good omen for the winning team.

Parrott and Jarrett have gone on to become one of the Winston Cup Series' great modern combinations, winning the Daytona 500 again in 2000, a superb follow-up to winning the NASCAR championship in the 1999 season.

THIS PAGE: Allied with Penske Motorsports and driver Rusty Wallace, Buddy Parrott built the team to beat in Winston Cup racing in 1993 and 1994. Wallace raced to eighteen wins in two seasons, far more than any other driver.
OPPOSITE PAGE, TOP: Todd Parrott's team was in peak form during the entire 1999 season. Their pit stops were swift, driver Dale Jarrett was in his best form, and the engines provided by team owner Robert Yates left the competition in the number 88 car's wake.
OPPOSITE PAGE, BOTTOM: In April 2001, Dale Jarrett (left) and Todd Parrott looked like they were on their way to another Winston Cup title. Here they've just won at Texas Motor Speedway. But by mid-season, difficulties had derailed their plans for the title.

THE Elliott *family*

It's difficult for many drivers to break into Winston Cup racing without having someone who can help crack open the door to NASCAR's elite division. But when Georgia's Elliott family entered the Winston Cup arena, they did it by smashing open the door as a family unit. Years later, the Winston Cup world was still reeling from the assault led by "Awesome Bill from Dawsonville."

Not that the path to NASCAR's top division was an easy one. When Dawsonville, Georgia, drivers Bill Elliott and his older brothers Dan and Ernie brought their Ford—owned by their father, George—to race against the big NASCAR stars beginning in 1976, they understandably struggled. But the family pulled together, and Bill's talents as a driver blossomed as Ernie's engine-building abilities were honed.

The family team fought to claim its handful of top-ten finishes each season, but by 1980 the struggle to win a race was still an ongoing campaign. To save money, up to twelve people would share a motel room, with Bill getting his own bed only on the night before a race.

In 1981, though, the family's fortunes finally began to take a turn for the better. After Bill crashed a car the family could ill afford to lose during a race in Michigan, auto parts manufacturer Harry Melling provided the team with desperately needed sponsorship. Impressed with the Elliott family's dedication and determination, as well as Bill's ability to run well even with inferior equipment,

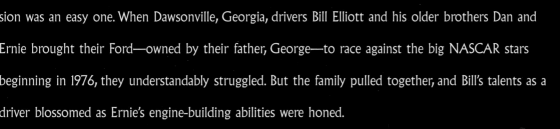

OPPOSITE PAGE: In well-organized campaigns, Bill Elliott's fans voted him Most Popular Driver so many times that, after the death of Dale Earnhardt in 2001, Elliott disqualified himself from the balloting so his old rival might win the award posthumously. THIS PAGE: A rare sight in 1989, as the Elliott crew attempts to diagnose a problem with the number 9 Thunderbird at Dover Downs International Speedway in Delaware. The Elliott team scored three wins and eight top-fives in the season.

THIS PAGE: Ernie Elliott (center), the engine-building master behind the Elliott team's powerful runs, stands by at South Carolina's Darlington Raceway in 1987. Ernie's motors pushed the team's Thunderbirds to six wins that year, and the championship in 1988.
OPPOSITE PAGE, TOP: Bill Elliott sits in his 1983 office—the cockpit of a Ford Thunderbird Winston Cup stock car. From this setting, Elliott won his first race in NASCAR's elite series, the

Melling bought the family team in 1982. With the weight of financial worries lifted, the Elliotts set about racing for real.

In 1983, at California's Riverside International Raceway road course, the Elliotts' dreams came true as Bill drove to their first win.

But the real fireworks came in 1985, when Elliott won eleven races. And by winning the Daytona 500, the Winston 500 at Alabama's Talladega Superspeedway, and the Southern 500 at South Carolina's Darlington Raceway in that single season, Bill Elliott won the Winston Million, a $1,000,000 bonus offered by the series sponsor. Bill immediately picked up a new nickname, "Million Dollar Bill."

In 1988, the Elliotts won just six races, but Bill's consistent runs combined with the victories brought the family team the Winston Cup championship. It was the first series title for Ford in nearly

twenty years.

In 1992, Bill Elliott surprised many when he left the Melling operation to drive for the famed Junior Johnson. As part of a two-car team, Elliott drove to five victories in the pair's first season together, but just a single victory came their way over the next two years. Feeling that the team was suffering from a lack of chemistry, Bill Elliott made plans to leave Johnson and reestablish an Elliott family–based racing team in 1995.

culmination of years of struggle and sacrifice.
OPPOSITE PAGE, BOTTOM: Firmly established as one of NASCAR's greatest stars and one of its most respected veterans, Bill Elliott was sought out by Chrysler program director Ray Evernham to be lead driver for Dodge's return to Winston Cup racing. Elliott responded by turning in the fastest qualifying lap in the season's first race, starting on the pole in the 2001 Daytona 500.

Proof that Elliott has always been one of NASCAR's best-known and best-loved drivers is that fans have voted him the Most Popular Driver award fifteen times in seventeen years.

That popularity and his great talent doubtless helped make Elliott the perfect choice as lead driver for Dodge's return to NASCAR Winston Cup racing in 2001, with brother Ernie spearheading engine development. Ray Evernham, who had left Hendrick Motorsports after helping guide Jeff Gordon to three championships, faced a formidable task in directing the development work that would lead Dodge back to NASCAR. He needed a reliable, established driver who could help decipher what the car was doing on the racetrack and determine a course of action to make it better.

Did Evernham's confidence in the Georgia driver pay off? On November 11, 2001, Bill Elliott drove his Dodge to victory lane at the Freedom 400—his first win since 1994—giving Evernham Motorsports its first Winston Cup victory.

N ot since the days of NASCAR's infancy—when Fonty, Tim, and Bob Flock all raced together—had race fans seen anything like it. Taking the green flag in Winston Cup races in 1992 were brothers Geoffrey, Brett, and Todd Bodine. The feat was made all the more remarkable by the fact that modern Winston Cup racing is incredibly competitive; to find three brothers all competing together at the same time is highly unusual.

Most Winston Cup drivers have traditionally honed their skills on the short tracks of the South, but when Geoffrey Bodine became the first of the three brothers to enter into the Winston Cup fray, he brought a background of racing in the brutally fierce Modified Series that competes throughout the Northeast. Renowned for tough racing among drivers who are equally tough, the Modified Series provided Bodine with an arsenal of skills and an attitude that helped him succeed in an environment of intense competition.

Geoffrey's first Winston Cup attempts came with eight starts in 1979 and 1981, yielding the young driver a single top-ten finish. Encouraged, Bodine took on the Winston Cup circuit seriously in 1982, winning Rookie of the Year honors with four top-fives among a total of ten finishes of tenth or better.

In 1984, Geoffrey hit his stride through an association with new Winston Cup car owner Rick Hendrick. The team scored three victories—at Martinsville, Virginia, at Nashville, Tennessee, and on the road course in Riverside, California. The New York driver was on his way.

One of the greatest honors of any Winston Cup driver's career came Geoffrey's way in 1986. He had suffered through a winless season in 1985, but had high hopes for 1986, buoyed by the strength

OPPOSITE PAGE: Geoff Bodine climbs a hill under hard cornering at Watkins Glen, New York, in 1991 Winston Cup Series action. The racing Bodine brothers grew up not far from Watkins Glen in the town of Chemung, New York.
THIS PAGE: When Junior Johnson shuttered his race team, he sold it to Brett Bodine, shown here behind the wheel at Bristol in 1998. While many drivers have failed at both owning a team and driving for it, Brett has successfully dealt with the dual role.

OPPOSITE PAGE, TOP: Early in the 1998 season, Todd Bodine (pictured here at the Charlotte Coca-Cola 600) looked to finally have the necessary tools at his disposal to succeed in Winston Cup racing with the number 35 car, but funding problems sent him back to the Busch Grand National Series.
OPPOSITE PAGE, BOTTOM LEFT: One of the most frightening crashes in NASCAR history took place on February 18, 2000. Geoff Bodine nearly lost his life competing in the NASCAR Craftsman Truck Series after getting airborne and tumbling down the front tri-oval at Daytona International Speedway.
OPPOSITE PAGE, BOTTOM RIGHT: Todd Bodine returned to the Winston Cup Series in 2001 as a teammate to Jimmy Spencer, one of brother Brett's fiercest rivals. Todd made the most of the opportunity, though, qualifying his number 66 car on the pole more than once.

of his car setup for the Daytona 500. Bodine qualified second fastest, and when the race got underway he passed pole sitter Bill Elliott and took over the lead on the third lap. Though other drivers also shared the lead during the race, it seemed that when he wanted to, Bodine could simply reassume first place. Late in the race, Bodine had pulled away from his challengers—except for Dale Earnhardt, who was drafting close behind. The fans were thrilled, on their feet with excitement—until, with three laps to go, Dale's Chevrolet ran out of gas. It was a bitter disappointment for Earnhardt, but a dream come true for Bodine, who cruised to an eleven-second victory in NASCAR's greatest race.

In 1990 and 1991, Bodine raced and won for legendary car owner Junior Johnson, then did the same for the great Bud Moore in 1992 and part of 1993. With fourteen wins to his credit through 1993, Bodine was looking for a new challenge. It came that year, when he bought the race team founded by Alan Kulwicki, the 1992 Winston Cup champion who had died in a plane crash in March. Bodine's purchase kept Alan's race team together as an entity, and in 1994 he won three races with his new team.

In 2000, tragedy struck. Geoffrey Bodine was involved in a horrific, nearly fatal crash while racing in NASCAR Truck Series competition at Daytona. Though he made a handful of Winston Cup starts later in the year, in early 2001 Geoffrey began to hint that his great career was coming to an end.

Geoffrey's younger brother Brett made his first Winston Cup start the year his brother won the Daytona 500. Like Geoffrey, Brett had raced through the Modified Series and then moved into NASCAR Busch competition, finishing as runner-up in the 1986 championship battle. He moved into Winston Cup full-time in 1988 with Bud Moore. In 1990, he began driving for drag-racing legend Kenny Bernstein. That association led to a Winston Cup victory for Brett at North Carolina's North Wilkesboro Speedway. After driving for Junior Johnson in 1995, Brett purchased the team from Johnson and has competed as an owner/driver since.

Brett's younger brother Todd also made his mark in the Busch Series after graduating from the Modified Series. Todd won his first Busch Series race in just his twenty-second start. In 1994, Todd took on the Winston Cup circuit full-time, racing for car owner Butch Mock. After showing very well at the Daytona 500—until he was caught up in an accident—Todd went on to score two top-five finishes during the rest of the season. Though the Mock association ended in 1995 with Todd returning to focus on the Busch Series, where he won frequently, in 2001 car owner Travis Carter gave Todd Bodine another shot at NASCAR's top division.

If Todd can find some of the opportunities to win that his brothers have enjoyed, he may very well become the third Bodine brother to add his name to the roster of Winston Cup winners.

THE
Wallace *Family*

L ike the members of the Bodine family, with their background in the Modified Series of the Northeast, the Wallaces first came to the Winston Cup Series from outside the confines of the Southern short-track world. Rusty Wallace, the first of three brothers to eventually begin competition in Winston Cup racing, cut his teeth in the Midwest-based American Speed Association.

Indeed, Rusty developed an extensive mental catalog of race car knowledge during his years in the

THIS PAGE: Mike Wallace, despite obvious racing talent, has struggled to break into the Winston Cup Series, competing behind the wheel of race cars fielded by lower-budget teams that have varied wildly in quality.
OPPOSITE PAGE: Rusty Wallace is one of the most intense competitors in the modern Winston Cup Series. But while some drivers leave decisions about stock car setups to the crew, Wallace's encyclopedic knowledge of chassis components and how they react gives him a competitive edge to complement his fiery desire to win.

ASA, and won the series championship in 1983. Prior to winning the ASA title, beginning in 1980, Rusty had made tentative forays into the Winston Cup Series, even scoring a runner-up finish in one of his nine starts. But Wallace concentrated solely on ASA racing the year he won the championship, bolstering his confidence before making his first attempt at a full-time Winston Cup career in 1984.

Driving a Pontiac for car owner Cliff Stewart, Wallace raced to two top-fives and four top-tens as he captured the Rookie of the Year title. After running one more season for Stewart, Rusty began an alliance with the Blue Max racing team of car owner Raymond Beadle in 1986.

At Tennessee's Bristol International Raceway on April 6, 1986, Rusty started in the middle of the field on the short, high-banked half-mile (0.8km) speedway. When the green flag waved, he mounted a determined charge toward the front. Wallace took over the lead as the race neared the halfway point, then stayed near the front of the pack. He took over again on lap 400, and remained out front to

beat Ricky Rudd and Darrell Waltrip. Not only was this Rusty Wallace's first Winston Cup Series win, it marked the first trip to victory lane for crew chief Barry Dodson. Rusty and Dodson combined for a second victory later that season at Virginia's Martinsville Speedway.

Wallace's career was solidly underway, and in 1987 he placed fifth in the season championship battle. The upward progress continued as the team raced to six victories in 1988, finishing just twenty-four points behind Bill Elliott's family team in the championship standings after winning four of the season's final events. Rusty could feel the title was within reach, and his team was one of the most respected in stock car racing.

They proved that point as the 1989 season got underway, scoring victories in three of the first six races. The wins at North Carolina Motor Speedway, Virginia's Richmond International Raceway, and Bristol Motor Speedway—a track that has been one of Rusty's favorites throughout his career—put Wallace at the top of the points standings. As the season wore on, his main competition for the title came into focus—Dale Earnhardt. But as Earnhardt experienced trouble late in the season, Rusty was coming on strong. Despite a difficult race in the season finale in Atlanta, Rusty Wallace held off Dale in the standings to become the 1989 NASCAR Winston Cup Series champion. The margin of victory was just twelve points.

In 1991, Wallace began a racing association with Roger Penske, the famous car owner who had helped Rusty early in the driver's career. With Penske, Rusty often was at the top of the points standings, and the victories came frequently, including ten in 1993 and eight in 1994.

Rusty Wallace reached a milestone in the 2000 season, scoring his fiftieth NASCAR Winston Cup Series career victory at the track where he had won his first, in Bristol, Tennessee

Rusty's younger brother, Kenny, began his own Winston Cup career in 1990 and 1991 with six starts over the two seasons. But Kenny's main focus was on gaining experience in the Busch Series, where he won for the first time at Florida's Volusia County Speedway in a car owned by Rusty.

Car owner Felix Sabates enticed Kenny with an offer to drive for him during the 1993 Winston Cup season, but the venture was not as successful as Kenny had anticipated, yielding just three top-ten finishes. He returned to the Busch Series, where he continued to win, then came back to Winston Cup racing for car owners Filbert Martocci, Andy Petree, and Jack Birmingham.

OPPOSITE PAGE, TOP: In 1980 young Rusty Wallace sports big hair, but more important were his big dreams. Determined to break into NASCAR's elite division, Wallace struggled to pay his dues.
OPPOSITE PAGE, BOTTOM: Hard work has paid off for Rusty (seen here zipping past bystanders at the Atlanta Cracker Barrel 500 in March 2001)—who has won millions of fans and earned the respect of his fellow racers. His competitive fire is one of the brightest in the Winston Cup Series.
THIS PAGE: The youngest Wallace brother, Kenny, has struggled to reach the pinnacle of NASCAR. His strong charges in the Busch Series have proven his abilities, but Kenny has yet to find the right opportunity in the Winston Cup Series.

In October 2000, Kenny played a role in Dale Earnhardt's final victory. Wallace placed himself behind the great champion late in the race, and the two drivers drafted through a congested pack of cars from mid-field to the front in just three laps in one of the most thrilling Winston Cup races ever.

Middle brother Mike Wallace is the final member of the racing Wallaces. Mike won hundreds of races on short tracks as he gained experience, leading up to his first Winston Cup start in 1991. His

first season-long attempt at Winston Cup success was in 1994, when he scored a single top-five finish driving for respected car owner Junie Donlavey. Later in the 1990s, he concentrated on racing in the NASCAR Truck Series, where he won numerous events.

In 2001, Mike returned to racing full-time in the Winston Cup Series, joining Rusty and Kenny in NASCAR's most competitive division.

number 43 at Dover in 1998) began competing for the Petty Enterprises team, it brought together the two most recognized names in American motorsports.

Mario Andretti is one of American auto racing's greatest names, and his legendary achievements in the Indianapolis 500 will certainly never be forgotten. Although he was an infrequent competitor in NASCAR's Grand National Series, Mario most definitely made his mark there as well.

In 1966, Andretti made four Grand National starts, including a thirty-seventh place run in the Daytona 500 for famed car builder Smokey Yunick. For the big NASCAR race in 1967, though, Mario switched from Yunick's Chevrolet to the powerful Ford team of Holman-Moody.

On February 26, 1967, Mario Andretti took the green flag of the Daytona 500 from a twelfth-place starting position, and quickly set sail for the lead. By lap twenty-three he was out in front, and eventually led the most laps of the race. But as has been seen many times in the history of stock car racing, leading the most laps doesn't guarantee a victory, and late in the race the fact that Mario was running low on fuel threatened Andretti's quest for the win. A late race caution flag proved to make the difference, allowing Mario to conserve his fuel supply and win the 1967 Daytona 500. It was a one-two sweep for Holman-Moody, as Fred Lorenzen was credited with second.

Mario Andretti never won again in NASCAR racing, but he had proven his ability to compete with stock car racing's greatest. While Mario's twin brother, Aldo, restricted his own racing to open-

In 1966 a young Mario Andretti was well known for his performances in the open cockpits of Indy cars long before he ever considered racing in stock cars. But when he did compete in NASCAR, he raced to win.

wheel competition, another member of Aldo's family would prove to follow a different path entirely.

Aldo's son, John, arrived in Winston Cup racing after experimenting with an assortment of motorsports. Since John had competed in everything from Indy cars to dragsters, there were many people who predicted Andretti's Winston Cup venture would be little more than another passing flirtation for the driver born in Bethlehem, Pennsylvania.

While growing up, John raced in go-kart competition, the early "classroom" for many racers. He later competed on local short tracks, getting his first seat time behind the wheel of stock cars. But Andretti moved on to the open-wheel midget cars of United States Auto Club in 1983, and seemed destined to share in his family's Indy racing heritage when he debuted in the CART series in 1987 with a sixth-place finish at Elkhart Lake, Wisconsin.

Yet John never seemed to find what he was looking for in the open-wheel series. After passing through road racing, off-road racing, and drag racing, he found himself driving in four Winston Cup races in 1993 for Billy Hagan. Of those four races, John finished only two.

In 1994, John was back with Hagan to start the season. In May, he attracted attention by running in the Indianapolis 500 and Coca-Cola 600 in the same day. Unfortunately, that was the only attention he was gaining, as he struggled to make a success out of a team suffering sponsorship woes. When the finances were not forthcoming, Andretti was forced to leave the foundering Hagan team and, in August, filled in at Petty Enterprises for the remainder of the season.

After an unsuccessful relationship with the Michael Kranefuss team in 1995 and into 1996, he traded places with Cale Yarborough Motorsports driver Jeremy Mayfield. Mayfield improved under the Kranefuss banner, but so did Andretti via his alliance with NASCAR legend Yarborough. On July 5, 1997, Andretti won on the same speedway where his uncle Mario had scored his greatest NASCAR win, Daytona International Speedway.

Richard Petty had been impressed during his association with John Andretti, and again by John's success with the Yarborough team. When sponsorship problems struck Cale's operation, Petty quickly moved to re-sign Andretti. John rewarded Petty's confidence by returning the Petty Enterprises team to victory lane at Virginia's Martinsville Speedway in 1999.

As one of the lead drivers for Dodge's return to Winston Cup racing, John Andretti is poised to continue to add to the legend of the Andretti family.

TOP: Unlike his cousin John, Mario's son Michael has never tested the NASCAR waters. Michael, seen here in 1985 receiving advice from Mario, has become a superstar in the CART open-wheel racing series.

BOTTOM: The thrill of winning a Winston Cup race for team owner Richard Petty (right) is clearly visible on John Andretti's face as he holds the day's trophy. The celebration took place after a convincing win at Virginia's Martinsville Speedway on April 18, 1999.

THE
Burton
family

Brothers Ward and Jeff Burton both began their professional racing careers on the same track, the famous paved oval at Virginia's South Boston Speedway. Both followed the same logical progression, moving up from South Boston to the NASCAR Busch Series, then on to the Winston Cup Series. That both brothers could not only find a home in NASCAR's top division, but also become proven Winston Cup winners, is a testament to their great driving talents.

Older brother Ward began racing at the age of eight, running in organized go-kart competition.

As a teenager, he moved on to stock car competition at South Boston. When he arrived in the NASCAR Busch Series in 1990, he was runner-up in the Rookie of the Year standings, bringing home three top-ten finishes. Though winless in 1991, in 1992 Ward broke through to the Busch victory lane with a strong run at North Carolina Motor Speedway. He backed that up the next season with three more wins.

His Busch team advanced to the Winston Cup Series in 1994, and though there were some promising moments—including a pole position at Charlotte Motor Speedway—the team struggled in 1995. Eventually, late in the season, Ward moved on to drive for car owner Bill Davis. It was a smart move. Within weeks of joining the Davis operation, Ward won his first Winston Cup race, at the same track where he had won his first Busch Series race, North Carolina Motor Speedway.

Burton's on-track association with Davis has been a fruitful one, including victories in 2000 and 2001 at South Carolina's Darlington Raceway. Away from the track, Ward has founded the Ward Burton

PREVIOUS PAGE: When the Dodge Intrepid heralded Chrysler's return to Winston Cup racing in 2001, Ward Burton—number 22—was one of the elite drivers selected to help bring the manufacturer back to motorsports prominence.
THIS PAGE: After finishing second to Dale Jarrett in the 2000 Daytona 500, Jeff Burton was determined to turn the tables when the series returned to Daytona on July 1. Here, Jeff, in car 99, holds off Jarrett and Rusty Wallace for his first win at the historic superspeedway.
OPPOSITE PAGE, TOP: The Burton brothers, Jeff (far left) and Ward (far right), prepare to race on the road course at Sears Point, California, in June 1999. Racing for well-respected teams and with major sponsorship, the Burtons were both threats to win.
OPPOSITE PAGE, BOTTOM: Dale Earnhardt and Mark Dinsmore attempt evasive maneuvers as Jeff Burton spins in the International Race of Champions competition. Though Jeff was surely disappointed by the accident, simply being invited to compete in the elite IROC series is a true racing honor.

Wildlife Foundation, which partners with other wildlife organizations to conserve wild lands and protect animal habitats. Jeff Burton followed older brother Ward's steps exactly to the professional stock car racing ranks, and actually entered Busch Series competition one year before Ward.

After wrapping up an impressive career at South Boston—featuring seven wins in twenty-one starts in 1988—Jeff broke into the Busch Series in 1989, and the next season won his first race, at Martinsville Speedway, in his home state of Virginia.

An offer to drive the Stavola Brothers entry in NASCAR's Winston Cup Series came Jeff's way in 1994, and he responded with two top-five finishes and the Rookie of the Year honors. Burton's strong runs in 1994 and 1995 attracted the attention of major Winston Cup team owner Jack Roush, who hired Jeff to campaign his Fords with teammate Mark Martin. The opportunity to learn from Martin while driving Roush's strong cars was ideal.

In 1996, Jeff managed six top-fives and improved to thirteenth in the season championship standings. He had come close to winning, and entered 1997 with confidence in his abilities, his crew's talents, and the calls of his crew chief, the famed Buddy Parrott. In 1997, at the inaugural Texas Motor Speedway race, Jeff Burton became a NASCAR Winston Cup winner. Having acquired a taste for winning, Jeff claimed two more victories that season.

As a key member of the powerful Roush Racing alliance, Jeff Burton has joined his brother as one of NASCAR's top stars, with fifteen victories through the 2000 season.

THE
Labonte
Family

While NASCAR's history is scattered with accounts of drivers who make aggressive charges through the pack, using a devil-may-care strategy in an attempt to power their way to victory lane, many of the most successful drivers of all time have followed a different, more conservative tack. The strategy in question involves taking care of the car as a race wears on, thereby keeping yourself in a position to win as the waving of the checkered flag draws near. Two Texans have become masters of this strategy in modern-day Winston Cup racing, brothers Terry and Bobby Labonte.

Terry, the elder brother born on November 16, 1956, cut his teeth on local tracks in Texas, and entered Winston Cup racing in 1978 driving for Louisiana car owner Billy Hagan. In 1980, Labonte won his first race, a hint of bigger things ahead. The 1984 season featured two victories and sixteen top-five finishes, making Terry the NASCAR Winston Cup champion. In high demand, Labonte moved to the Junior Johnson team for three years, beginning in 1987, and won races in each of those seasons.

While Terry went winless in 1990 and 1991, his brother Bobby began to attract attention by winning the 1991 NASCAR Busch Series championship

THIS PAGE: With the motorsports resources of Hendrick Racing and the financial backing of a major sponsor, Terry Labonte could smile over his return to championship form. OPPOSITE PAGE: The bright green stock cars of the Joe Gibbs Racing stable first gained fame with Dale Jarrett behind the wheel, but it was Bobby Labonte who took the team to the coveted Winston Cup championship.

ABOVE LEFT: The road-course skills of Terry Labonte (in the number 11 car) are put to the test at Watkins Glen in 1987 as he battles one of the best road racers, Rusty Wallace. ABOVE RIGHT: Consistency in the pits was a key component in Terry's quest for the 1996 Winston Cup championship. His Hendrick Motorsports crew was among the best.

and nearly repeating the feat in 1992. Car owner Bill Davis noticed the younger Labonte's talents, and hired him to run in Winston Cup competition in 1993. After learning the ropes with Davis, Bobby began 1995 with the race team of former NFL coach Joe Gibbs.

Meanwhile, Terry had endured three winless seasons driving once again for Bill Hagan, before signing up with the powerful Rick Hendrick racing team. Terry responded to his new team by winning three times in 1994 and three times in 1995. That set the stage for a glorious 1996 season, when two victories and a string of consistent runs brought Terry the NASCAR Winston Cup championship for a second time.

Two of the notable events in Terry Labonte's great Winston Cup career are inexorably linked with the legendary Dale Earnahrdt, and both took place at tiny Bristol Motor Speedway.

The high-banked half-mile (0.8km) track is notorious for furious action, and the August night race in 1997 had been no exception as the Winston Cup drivers edged toward the closing laps. Terry Labonte had used his considerable skills as a short-track driver to place his Chevrolet out front, but the black Monte Carlo of Dale Earnhardt was close behind in second.

As the white flag waved, the cars roared around the tiny track for the final time. Labonte clung to the lead, Earnhardt clung to Labonte's tail bumper. Then, coming through the final turn, Earnhardt tapped Labonte with enough force that Labonte's car went spinning. Yet such was Terry's momentum that his car crossed the finish line ahead of Dale, despite the fact that his stock car was out of control in mid-crash. The image of Labonte's number 5 Chevrolet pulling into victory lane, its nose crushed and spewing clouds of steam from a shattered radiator, is a sight Terry's fans will always remember and cherish.

The same scenario was played out again two years later. The white flag was waving, Labonte was leading, Earnhardt was in pursuit. But there was one dramatic difference—this time the contact with Dale came exiting turn two. The finish line was too far away for Terry to slide across this time, and on this night it was the Earnhardt fans who rejoiced.

Race fans also have a certain memory of Bobby Labonte at Bristol—the young driver angrily hurling his helmet at his crashed race car, an act of pure frustration. But that was just part of Bobby's learning process, and as the seasons passed his racing maturity began to show. Labonte learned the lesson his brother already knew well—you can't win championships unless you not only win races, but finish well in the races you can't win.

By the end of the 1999 season, Bobby's team was reaching that level of consistency. With a dozen career wins and a second-place finish in the championship standings, Labonte and his team looked to 2000 with excitement.

From the beginning of the year 2000, Bobby Labonte was at the top of the points standings. By mid-season, it looked like the championship battle would come down to a fight between Bobby and his brother's old Bristol nemesis, Dale Earnhardt. Bobby Labonte won races in 2000, four of them, but when he wasn't winning he was finishing in the top five or top ten. Bobby hit his stride, consistently performing well race after race. And that was the difference that led to the Winston Cup championship for Bobby Labonte, coming in 265 points ahead of Earnhardt.

Terry and Bobby Labonte—brothers and Winston Cup champions. The Labontes are the only brothers ever to achieve that feat, the ultimate example of the power of family tradition in NASCAR's elite series.

ABOVE LEFT: The celebration begins after Bobby Labonte swept to victory in the last race of the 1999 season at Atlanta Motor Speedway. The win ensured Bobby's ranking as runner-up in the final points standings.
ABOVE RIGHT: Being a two-time Winston Cup champion guarantees popularity with the race fans. Here Terry obliges another autograph request.

BIBLIOGRAPHY

Fielden, Greg. *Forty Years of Stock Car Racing.* **Volumes 1–4.**
Myrtle Beach: Galfield Press, 1988, 1989, 1990.

———. *Forty Years of Stock Car Racing: Forty Plus Four.*
Myrtle Beach: Galfield Press, 1994.

——— and Golenbock, Peter. *Stock Car Racing Encyclopedia.*
New York: Macmillan, 1997.

Moriarty, Frank. *Sunday Drivers: NASCAR Winston Cup Stock Car
Racing.* Charlottesville: Howell Press, 1994.

———. *Supercars: The Story of the Dodge Charger Daytona and
Plymouth SuperBird.* Charlottesville: Howell Press, 1996.

———. *The Encyclopedia of Stock Car Racing.* New York:
MetroBooks, 1998.

———. *Superstars of Stock Car Racing.* New York: MetroBooks,
1999.

———. *Dale Earnhardt.* New York: MetroBooks, 2000.

———. *Dale Jarrett.* New York: MetroBooks, 2000.

Various. *NASCAR Winston Cup Series Media Guides.* Winston-
Salem: Sports Marketing Enterprises, various seasons.

CREDITS

INDEX